On Love

Life is love in action!
Ed Scott

On Love

A Happy Heart

Ed Scott

On Love: A Happy Heart

© 2016 Ed Scott

Published and distributed in the United States by CreateSpace, an Amazon.com company.

All rights reserved. This book may not be used or reproduced by any means—graphic, electronic, or mechanical, including photocopying, recording, and taping—or by any information storage retrieval system without the written permission of the author or publisher.

Because of the dynamic nature of the Internet, any web addresses or links contained in this book may have changed since publication and may no longer be valid. The views expressed in this work are solely those of the author and do not necessarily reflect the views of the publisher, and the publisher hereby disclaims any responsibility for them.

ISBN-13: 9781539336235
ISBN-10: 1539336239

Also by Ed Scott

Wisdom of the Heart: Create Your Own Reality

Life Is about Choices: Creating Our Reality

Quantum Consciousness: Who Do You Think You Are?

God Says Hello: A Quantum Reality

I Think Therefore It Is: Beliefs Create Reality

www.aquantumreality.com

Dedication

This book is dedicated to my beloved wife Ruth. Ruth was love personified. Family, friends, associates, and all who met her were enriched by the depth of her knowledge and her caring, loving ways. By example, Ruth taught me, and many others, that our life's stories are written moment by moment in how we've loved, in things we've shared, and in the ways we've touched each other's hearts.

After a courageous struggle with cancer, Ruth died in September of 2016 while I was writing this book. Some of the quotations I found in her old diary are used at the end of each chapter in this book. This beautiful woman will continue to inspire others and will be remembered for a very long time by so many people.

Think not that you can guide the course of love; for love, if it finds you worthy, shall guide your course.

—Khalil Gibran

Table of Contents

Preface · xi

Chapter 1	Wisdom of the Heart · · · · · · · · · · · · · · · · · ·	1
Chapter 2	Know Who You Are. · · · · · · · · · · · · · · · · · ·	7
Chapter 3	Life Is About Choices · · · · · · · · · · · · · · · · ·	28
Chapter 4	Our Beliefs Create Reality · · · · · · · · · · · · · ·	41
Chapter 5	The Happy Universe · · · · · · · · · · · · · · · · · ·	50
Chapter 6	Love and Beauty ·	58
Chapter 7	Beliefs and Quantum Reality · · · · · · · · · · · ·	66
Chapter 8	The Mind and Consciousness · · · · · · · · · · · ·	69
Chapter 9	It's About Time ·	86
Chapter 10	The Law of Attraction · · · · · · · · · · · · · · · ·	98
Chapter 11	Subjective or Objective Reality · · · · · · · · · · ·	108
Chapter 12	Meditation and Mindfulness · · · · · · · · · · · · ·	117
Chapter 13	Body, Mind and Spirit · · · · · · · · · · · · · · · ·	125

Epilogue · 139
About the Author · 141

Preface

Have you ever been head-over-heels in love? Can you recall having felt so alive and exuberant that your heart was about to burst with happiness? Did that special someone steal your heart? Steal your mind, or both? Our sensation of being immersed in love with another being is a phenomenon of life-altering energies of our heart and minds. Were you delighted to see that special person after an absence, and wish that you could be with them all of your waking moments? Love, it seems, is not a rational state of mind.

For centuries, humankind has studied the nature of human existence and pondered reality and the purpose of life on this planet. After studying the human condition and our consciousness, we have come to realize that our reality should be better than our dreams. It all begins with our beliefs and a happy loving heart. Love and happiness are not a destination to arrive at, but the path and a key to our purpose on this earth.

There have been knowledgeable visionary writers who have set the stage and inspired countless others to perform and thrive in their roles in life. Some of these writers and teachers are social architects because of the impact of their powerful words. Many of them exhibit a supernatural awareness and prophetic vision. These are the writers and guides that have contributed greatly to my knowledge. Their knowledge and experience can help guide each of us in learning more about ourselves and the world in which we live.

Many of us have studied poetry, comparative religions, esoteric writings, various philosophies, metaphysics, and other supportive sciences. My travels throughout the world have provided me the invaluable experience of observing various cultures, values, and belief systems as I searched for answers to my many questions. After more than forty years of observation, study, and research, I have joined the growing movement of people who believe that an open, loving heart will see what our eyes cannot. I am further convinced that our human evolution requires that we know our beliefs and our human capabilities. We are destined to evolve and to realize that we determine our own life experiences with our unique personalities. Our individual beliefs and daily experiences are relevant to life in the modern quantum world and it is our human consciousness that drives evolution. We are meant to be happy in maximizing our human potential and love is the ultimate answer.

While many other books can transport you to magical realities of illusion and fiction, I prefer to challenge your beliefs with knowledge and inspire you to reach a higher level of awareness of the wonders of our human reality. Consider the reading this book as an experience in and of itself. I realize that written words lack the persuasion of a verbal discussion and are thereby subject to possible misinterpretation. The following chapters are meant to prompt experiences far beyond the reading of another person's words in a book. I invite you to identify your core beliefs and values and to enhance your life in a decisive way by creating your intentional reality with a happy, loving heart. Creating reality intentionally will contribute to the growing body of knowledge and to the global human experience.

It is not by accident that you are here on earth. Many people believe incorrectly that we are humans destined to seek a spiritual experience, when the reverse is actually true. We are spiritual, energy beings experiencing our unique and separate roles in the drama of human life. The extent to which we will create and change our realities will depend upon our levels of awareness, our beliefs, and our commitment to change. This book is written to provide you with a better understanding of why you are here and what you need to learn and with an understanding of how you can share your talents and gifts with others. Knowledge of your true identity and a happy, meaningful purpose in life are both readily available. I am humbled by what I have learned and am grateful for the opportunity to share this writing with you. Thank you.

> *You are here to enable the divine purpose of the universe to unfold. That is how important you are.*
>
> —Eckhart Tolle

I
Wisdom of the Heart

There is a wisdom of the heart that provides deep understanding and insight learned from our most memorable events, our most emotional times, and our closest personal relationships. In this age of an evolving higher consciousness, we should look to love and beauty in sharing the human experience with others, heart to heart. It was Voltaire who stated, "I have chosen to be happy, it's good for my health." A happy heart is also a healthy heart. In Proverbs 15:13, New American Standard Bible is written, "A happy heart makes the face cheerful."

The human heart is a marvelous organ. It is actually a muscle. This important organ has often been portrayed as the center of emotion in our bodies. Hence, the often-used expressions of *heartfelt*, *heartless*, *heartrending*, *have a heart*, and so forth. The body chakra system also describes the human heart as having an autonomous and measurable energy circuit. According to the Institute of HeartMath, Dr. J. Andrew Armour introduced the term *heart-brain* in 1991. Research has now shown that our human hearts have a heart-brain composed of more than forty thousand neurons that can sense, feel, learn, and remember. The independent heart-brain can exchange messages with our cranial brain about how the body feels and handles our experiences. More often than not, we will make better decisions from the heart rather than the brain. Consider too, that unconditional love emanates from the human heart and is recognized by the human mind.

According to documentary filmmaker David Malone, in his film *Of Hearts and Minds*, the human heart is an organ of truth and emotion. Sayings such as "I love you with all my heart" and "My heart swelled with joy" are based upon something biologically real and true. Our brains and hearts work together symbiotically in producing and recognizing emotions, and our hearts contain the same neurons found clustered in the right ventricle of our brains. Neurons are required for the brain to form thoughts. Our heart-brain is always at work when we experience fear, love, compassion, and empathy for the feelings of others. On the other hand, intense negative emotions can put our hearts at risk for heart attacks.

Incredibly, the measured electrical fields of our hearts are much stronger than that of our brains. Our heart-brain is a complex network of neurons, neurotransmitters, proteins, and support cells. The heart is coherent with the cranial brain when we experience sincere positive emotions. The heart processes these emotions, and our heart rhythms then become coherent and harmonious. The human heart speaks from genuine feelings and authenticity, while our brains and our minds know opinions and fears. The voice of our hearts will offer intuition and a feeling of common sense. Our happiness is a product of the heart that is recognized by the brain. An example of the human heart speaking is the expression of gratitude and appreciation registered in the human heart. A happy heart is also a grateful heart. Our sense of genuine gratitude sends a powerful message from our hearts to our brains and body systems and balances our physiologies with heart rhythms that are coherent or harmonious with our brains. Also remember that those opinions, ideas, fears, and other emotions are our own creations as well and are not always reliable or under our self-control. It is well ordered that we should be conscious, happy, loving beings.

Hugging one another is a happy experience. Our hugging one another will boost self-esteem. Hugging shows that people are loved and considered special. Hugs relax muscles, release body tensions, and increase circulation in the body's tissues. Hugs allow us to both give and receive and show us that love flows both ways. The energy exchanged in a hug encourages empathy and promotes respect. Also, without words, hugs—the miracle drug—can express love. Let me quote the following words of Marcus Julian Felicetti: "Research has shown that the act of hugging is extremely effective in healing sickness, disease, loneliness, depression, anxiety, and stress. The nurturing touch of a hug builds trust and a sense of safety. Holding a hug for an extended period of time lifts one's serotonin levels, elevating mood and creating happiness. Hugs can also instantly boost oxytocin levels, which dispel feelings of loneliness, isolation, and anger. Hugs strengthen the immune system and stimulate our thymus glands to regulate and balance the body's production of white blood cells to keep us healthy and disease free."

Happiness is a prelude to joy, and laughter is a cause for much happiness in our lives. Laughter is a natural human response and an experience of our own making in our experienced reality. We should then enjoy laughter often for happier and healthier lives. Happy hearts and happy faces make for very happy places.

Laughter is a very powerful and pervasive phenomenon of psychological, emotional, and physical proportions. Laughter may often be experienced involuntarily, uncontrollably, and even contagiously. It doesn't take much to begin feeling the benefits of laughter or humor. Laughing is fun, makes us feel better, and is healthy for us. The happiness that comes from laughter can be experienced often and by nearly everyone. Children, especially infants, are the most frequent benefactors of laughter. It is significant to also notice that most children are relatively free of worry in their preteen years. I have a small cloth beanbag doll that giggles and laughs uncontrollably and it sounds much like a small child or infant. When I squeeze this toy, within seconds I experience my own uncontrollable, contagious laughter triggered in response to the googly-eyed beanbag doll. All previous thoughts, concentrations, and stresses instantly vanish, leaving us happy and relaxed.

From the medical standpoint, laughing increases our endorphins and dopamine in addition to increasing muscle relaxation and reducing pain. Laughter reduces stress, anxiety, and depression. Laughing out loud, being amused, and even anticipating something funny can lead to positive emotions and happiness. Laughter helps to form close bonds with family, friends, and others because laughter is universally recognized. Laughter and humor make us more attractive to others and enhance our marriages and other close, loving relationships. Happy, positive people are fun to be around. Because we are energy beings, those people with higher frequencies and greater positive energies will entrain and raise those with lower energy frequencies.

Similar to laughter, smiles and smiling play a pleasant and important role in our lives. If we smile five or more times each day for no reason at all, it will improve our health. Smiling not only causes our bodies to produce endorphins, but smiles are also a most positive communication and friendly greeting of love. Smiles communicate physical, mental, and spiritual health. It requires sixty-two facial muscles to frown but only twenty-six to smile. So smile; it increases your face value. Embrace love's smile as wisdom of the heart.

The Buddhist tradition can teach us much regarding happiness, joy, and a loving kindness. The tenets, or principles, of Buddhism have withstood the test of time. The Buddhist tradition follows four basic principles in discovering, identifying and abandoning the human ego in order to find spiritual enlightenment. The Buddhists believe that we must meet the ego head-on in order to control and direct it.

The first aspect is that of loving-kindness. Learn to think lovingly of all others and of all things. This truly is an unconditional love that is both a feeling and an intentional action. We are all connected, in thought, vibratory energy, and spirit. Even if at first we cannot feel lovingly toward others, we can learn to show kindness to all. Then love and understanding will follow. Love does not know competition, righteous equality, power, or control. Genuine kindness is much more than a social courtesy or consideration. Kindness is a willful sharing with other people and other creatures with no strings attached. Kindness should begin with us as kindness shared promotes unity and the feeling of love. Kindness is also the twin to compassion and presents the simplicity of love with tenderness and gentleness. We can learn to love all of our creation. In creating our reality, we become cocreators with a happy heart and peaceful mind.

The second aspect, or tenet, is that of joy. We should fully appreciate joy when we experience it and learn to find happiness in all things at all times. Happiness is a prelude to joy, and joy can promote the abandonment of fear. It's not so easy when we are fearful, uncertain, or upset, but with practice, we can eliminate fear and doubt. We also learn to be comfortable with unexpected surprises, fears, losses, and other unsettling emotions. Risk and fear dissolve into faith, and our expectations become a joyous reality.

A third aspect is that of compassion. Compassion begins by empathizing with others because we truly care about their well-being. We can learn to care about others more than is normally believed to be wise. Compassion is a sympathetic consciousness for the suffering and plights of others. Compassion is a true understanding and sharing of their pain and emotional distress.

Freedom, the fourth aspect, means a freedom of the mind. Freedom of the mind requires practice in being completely open and honest—first with ourselves and then with others. Fearlessness is part of freedom. Fear is the byproduct of our ego and is the root cause of hatred, prejudice, and other unwanted, defensive thoughts and practices. Without fear, we can learn to dream the impossible and find that anything is possible. Love dissolves fear, and the entire universe appears differently when seen through the eyes of love.

To live a happy and contented life we will need to know who we are and our capabilities; you are the most important person that you could ever wish to know.

Wisdom begins with a loving heart.

—Thomas Carlyle

II

Know Who You Are.

Not so long ago in India, a wise old Yogi heard a knock on the door to his hut. "Who's there?" he asked. After a few seconds and yet another knock at his door, the Yogi again asked, "Who is there?" And yet again there was no answer. After several minutes, a third knock was heard at the door. Now exasperated, the learned Yogi threw open the door to find a humble man outside. "I have asked twice who you are. Why have you not answered me?" said the Yogi. The humble man replied and said, "If I knew who I was, I would not be knocking at your door, seeking that advice."

Even today, there are countless people who are uncertain about whom they really are. And there are many more people who are mistaken in their beliefs about whom they really are and the relationships that they have with the universe. Moreover, the same people will not likely be aware that their dominant thoughts and beliefs are the creative force of their realities. We must first know ourselves in order to be happy in our earthly experience. Our personal beliefs will affect our state of happiness and our experience of being unhappy.

Imagine for a moment what would happen if we were to suffer amnesia from a sudden fall or head injury. Our faculty of memory is the key to our identity and to holding on to that which we love, who we are, and anything else that we wish never to lose. What would our identity be without any memory of our name, history, development, beliefs, behaviors, and life choices? Would we not create a new persona? Our life would never again be the same, and we would have little choice but to begin to question our identity in a surreal but interactive and virtual world. We would be very much aware of our being and our instincts but we would necessarily question our new environment. Was that forgotten life a created interactive and virtual reality as viewed and experienced by our true being? Without memory, there would be no identity, values, or beliefs for us to build upon or change.

What would it take now, today, to alter your beliefs that have been formulated for years by our structured society? When we examine the fabricated historical structures of our virtual reality we can begin to understand how we have formed our basic self-recognition. Virtual reality is a simulated, interactive, and three-dimensional environment that can be experienced in a seemingly real manner in an artificial world. Virtual does not mean fake or unreal but an experience of being real without actually being real. It becomes quickly apparent that we create our reality. Furthermore, we challenge our own beliefs and often decide upon a new set of beliefs because of new information or new perspectives. Our evolving, changing beliefs shape our changing reality. The challenge of self-realization is to find and define our true selves that remain the same despite our changing reality.

Are you aware of your naturally happy heart? What is it that defines you? Who do you think you are? More importantly, who do you *know* that you are with certainty? Do you know how you have been involuntarily programmed and defined since birth in this illusionary world? Do you know how this programming occurred? And do you know who you are beyond a mental and physical description? If you are seeking a meaningful happy life, do you wish to reach self-realization? Set aside your judgments, your assumed knowledge, and your beliefs long enough to consider what millions of others are discovering when they look beyond the physical realm. Learn how our dominant thoughts and beliefs are the creative force of quantum reality and happiness. The most beautiful things in life are those seen and felt with our heart. We should do that which makes us happy, be with those who make us smile, and love as long as we live.

An interesting aspect arises in considering who we are as individuals. A news article published in February 2012 by the American Association of Retired Persons (AARP) detailed the recent study entitled the "Five Top Regrets of the Dying." AARP staff interviewed people who worked in palliative care and hospice care. These workers tended and spoke with many elderly and dying patients. The interviews showed that the most common regret reported by all patients was this: "I wish that I'd had the courage to live a happy, satisfying life true to myself, not the life others and society expected of me." The interesting aspect of their regrets is that in creating their life experiences, many people abandoned their dreams and aspirations because they lacked the courage to insist upon a fulfilled life. Who they believed they were very often became hijacked, and a new and random reality overtook them. Those patients had been expected to exercise discretion and compromise their goals, and they failed to establish a life of their own beliefs and choosing.

Many others found a sense of community and personal security in a life prescribed by the church. Free souls now trapped, they were hostages within their bodies with many unfulfilled expectations. Sadly, they were not free to explore and experience the vastness and the freedom of their true beings. Organized religions tell us that we were born with original sin, unclean, and unhappy without the forgiveness of the church. These idioms are only agreements in moral codes and practices.

Our personalities are a collection of certain qualities or aspects that determine and shape our physical and mental bodies and minds. We know more about our physical bodies than we know of our spiritual essence. It is the healthy spiritual experience and the growth of our consciousness that is the purpose of our lives.

Our personal body—or earthly body—moves along in a horizontal time and space continuum, but our spiritual energy bodies grow and ascend vertically. Our personality, complete with our ego, is but the first and lowest level of our reality, which is sometimes called *the physical level*. From a nonphysical reality, the higher soul will search for something far beyond the realm of our senses, space, time, matter, linguistics and religious beliefs. A multisensory human being will evolve with a personality that recognizes, understands, and aligns with the energy and nonlocal dynamics of the soul. Moreover, our personality-to-soul communication is the experience of our higher self, which is our spiritual self. Our higher selves have no reason to not be happy and loving as we create our unique realities.

Our real selves are immortal and may revisit an earthly role over several lifetimes for spiritual learning and growth. Many people believe that our souls reside within our physical bodies. According to the New American Standard Bible, in Genesis 2:7, the religious definition of the word *soul* is "a human body brought to spiritual life by the breath of God." Common expressions and songs speak of the heart and soul as physiological organs. It is also believed by countless people that our consciousness is our soul and that it is located within either our hearts or our heads at the third-eye center. Still others believe that our human awareness within our minds is that of the soul. However, human consciousness requires no thought. Most likely our conscious being is our soul—an immaterial and spiritual essence that is part of the infinite cosmos that embodies the temporal human body. Many people refer to the soul as our higher self, our true, original being. C. S. Lewis has said that we don't have a soul. We are a soul using the human body. Our consciousness is an energy form that flows within, through and around our bodies—much like an aura. Like the air or ether that we breathe, consciousness is without dimension and melds with the consciousness of the universe. We are all composite pieces of the body, mind, spirit, and universe. Elements of our earthly bodies can be traced to exploded stars and stardust in an electromagnetic cosmos.

In recent years, physicists have proven that our universe is a large realm of energy that repeatedly flashes in and out of being in nanoseconds. It is a virtual reality. There is nothing truly solid in our cosmos. Even our television sets and electronic games display millions of bouncing electrons, creating the illusion of form and motion. The universe is a field—or matrix—of consciousness, intelligence, matter, and energy. The intelligent element of the universe depends upon consciousness and electromagnetic energy. The other element in the universe is matter. Matter is nothing more than energy in slow motion—vibratory frequencies derived from consciousness. The construction of all matter and light is done by the resonance of frequencies that govern molecular movement. With our conscious and thought energies we create the frequency resonance required to create matter.

Intelligence without energy is powerless, and energy includes power and force. Matter, or mass, includes form, pattern, and structure. It is known that everything in the universe is electromagnetic energy and information, although information is not synonymous with intelligence. Consciousness does not arise from matter but creates matter.

Now, notice that our human elements correspond to those of the universe: matter, energy, intelligence, and consciousness. So now who do you think you are? We were made in the image of a creative universe. The consciousness of all living organisms is part of the universal ether as we are all one in nature and essence. It has also been determined that the universal ether is within all things as consciousness, energy, matter, and intelligence. Together, we are also a global community of particle matter and energy.

Because all energy is electromagnetic in nature, everything that happens in our bodies is an electromagnetic exchange between cells. The entire cosmos and our smaller universe are comprised of electromagnetic energies. On the smaller physical scale, every atom has a vibratory frequency and all plant and animal bodies are bio-electric energy forms subject to the Laws of the Universe. The resonant frequency of all matter is what provides life, evolution or growth, change or transformation, and manifestation. To better know ourselves, we should realize that there are four basic ways in which imbalance and disease are created in the human body. The first is through toxic substances that we consume. The second is by the pollution that we breathe, and thirdly, by exposure to negative energy environments. The fourth cause of disease and imbalance is the manner in which we think and our emotional impacts. It becomes very obvious that human consciousness, awareness, and our human volition create and direct our lives and our experiences. We are bio-electrical-magnetic creatures operating in, and experiencing an electromagnetic environment. When electromagnetic activity ceases, physical life ceases on this planet.

In our global community, it is only with our human awareness and our minds that we separate one body from another. It all happens within our heads. Even though our brains cannot see outside of our skulls, it is our minds that are the matrix and the key to accessing the quantum universe. Further yet, with our intention, our minds create our reality and our separate and unique roles in life. Why not a happy role in this life? Our consciousness manifests in the physical body, and we use our physical attributes to experience our creation and the higher aspects of our beings. Our dominant thoughts, words, intentions, and actions all have the power of creation. Continuously evolving and growing in self-actualization, we construct exactly who and what we are after birth with genetic traits influenced from our previous lives. Our dominant thoughts and beliefs provide an opportunity to evolve and become what we truly wish to be in self-actualization. Like a reflective mirror, our relationships with all things and persons allow us to observe what we are becoming. Wherever we are, we should be there fully. Our realities are our own unique creation and our experience; we own it in total awareness of our higher spiritual self.

Consider the beauty that we see in a rose in bloom. The beauty that we see is a mirror reflection of the self and our creation. The same is true of other people and experiences. Without other people, things, and events, we would not and could not have experiences of reality. We create everything visible and invisible in order to have and enjoy our experience and to further adjust or change our cause and effect. Those created people, relationships, and experiences will define us if and when we react to the words and actions of others. As conscious, loving beings, we should learn to open both our minds and our hearts to others because they are part of our creation. The relationships that we have created and attracted to our lives at any moment are exactly the ones that we need in our lives at that moment. Everyone who has entered, left, or remained in our lives has been there for a reason and purpose at the proper time. Our lives eventually cease and no one gets out of it alive. But where, then, do we go?

Because our lives are nonlocal events, there is no place for us to get to. We don't have to go anywhere. Our beliefs, behaviors, and decisions are a portrait of who we are in this earthly experience. Our thoughts are a direct experience of our own fabrication. The afterlife too, will be an experience of our own making. Everything in this earthly realm and that of the next, are of our individual creation. Even this book is a created autobiographical with regard to my beliefs and behaviors because it reflects my reality, and it may possibly change your experience or beliefs in one way or another. In a small way, I have now become a part of your creation, and you are certainly now a part of my reality. With coincidence, or synchronicity, we have created this happening.

There is a creative force and divine intelligence in our universe that responds to our reasonable requests for nearly anything. Our elegant universe contains everything that we need to know in order to acquire peace, joy, love, beauty, health, wealth, knowledge, and an increased awareness. There are many unseen and not-yet-fully-understood forces and powers in our universe that can enable us to raise our human awareness and consciousness to our full potential. We need only to ask and to offer a sincere thank you when we have been obliged. Both our asking and our thanks are fervent prayers to the creative source of our universe. They are a wireless connection.

Both the ancient Greek philosopher and scientist Socrates and his student Plato referred to the universal ether as the *aether* and called it the fifth element—in addition to earth, air, fire, and water. Even today, the fifth element is believed by some to be that which connects our thoughts to a universal consciousness. Some scientists refer to the ethereal element as the "zero-point field." They further believe that this universal ether contains visible matter, dark energy, and dark matter. Remember that our human brains are electrical fields that emanate and direct our thought energies. We are energy beings operating within an energy world and environment. The universal ethereal field transmits and carries all forms of energies. The electrical fields of our brains and our bodies are but very small blips in the vast energy field of the universe. Actually, the human brain is the matrix and the source of all matter and creation. Consider that quantum theory is not about the behavior of matter but about our knowledge and use of such behavior.

There are several studies and articles currently describing multisensory perception and its impact on humanity. For centuries, our awareness of our human capacity for perception has been limited to one modality—the modality of the five senses in the physical world. Our sensory perception is only the second of four levels of experienced reality. Our multisensory awareness now recognizes and includes the perception of nonphysical information via our capacity for intuition, telepathy, and synchronicity in the vast universal field of knowledge. Each of us has perhaps known individuals who possess and utilize clairvoyance and clairaudience. Clairvoyance is the human faculty of perceiving things and events beyond our normal sensory contacts. Those persons who are prescient are described as having or showing knowledge of events before these events take place. Clairaudience is the human perception of hearing that which is inaudible to our normal range of hearing. These higher senses allow us to access information and wisdom not available through the use of our rational minds. As multisensory beings, we should challenge the collective and interactive human patterns of power, control, and fear and promote higher awareness, wisdom, cooperation, and love. Our awareness of our intentions will hold us responsible for our thoughts, words, and actions, which are the means for our spiritual evolution.

Multisensory perception seamlessly integrates with and supports our physical and sensory perceptions. According to author Gary Zukav in his 1989 book *The Seat of the Soul*, multisensory perception has been described as one of the largest evolutionary advances in humanity. A new species of human beings is being created from within the many thousands of us to facilitate an expanded collective global consciousness. We need to expand our perceptions and human awareness beyond the level of our five bodily senses. There have always been a limited number of persons with multisensory perception; however, as our collective human awareness increases, a growing number of people are acquiring a higher and more evolved consciousness.

The electrical energy of our human brains can easily be measured with today's sciences, and Kirlean photography has shown the most intense energy is around our head and our hands. According to *Wikipedia*, Kirlean photography is a photographic technique used to capture the phenomenon of electric discharges from the human body. For many centuries, healers have been aware of and have used the energy emanating from their hands to perform body-healing techniques.

Quantum physics involves the Planck level—the smallest of the small—and has shown that the ether transmits and facilitates all energies and particles of matter. In a subsequent chapter, we shall see how the universal laws govern our universe. The ether is a receptive, vibrating medium. The unified field also conducts and manages all of the forces and matter in the universe. At a subatomic level, bosons and gluons carry the four basic forces that move or transmit wave and particle matter. The seven Universal Laws also govern the nature of our cosmos. The ether, or plasma, includes a dark energy that pervades all things and serves to conduct and carry powerful energies faster than light speed over great distances.

The science of theoretical physics proposes that everything in our universe consists of vibratory energy as described in the Universal Law of Vibration. Energy is constantly vibrating and spinning but never created or destroyed. It helps to understand, in accordance with Einstein's theory of relativity, that energy can be turned into matter, and vice-versa according to author Brian Greene in his book *The Elegant Universe*. Light, sound, solids, liquids, and body tissue—all things are comprised of energy, according to science. All things are made of energy vibrating at different wavelengths and spinning on the matrix of the space-time fabric. For example, those things that appear to be solid are not truly solid but are vibrating at a slower wavelength. Even the four forces in nature are comprised of vibrating and spinning elements. Albert Einstein's formula of energy equals mass (position) times velocity (momentum) proposes that everything in the cosmos is a form of measurable energy. Like a pebble creates vibrations that appear as ripples in a body of water, our thoughts create vibrational energies that travel outward in the universe to attract same or similar vibrations that manifest events in our lives.

Time is the gatekeeper of change because time accompanies both matter and energy. Time also traps all things physical. Take away time and space and matter will not exist—poof, we will disappear! Because of the element of that which we call time, it is impossible to know or measure both the locality and velocity of matter simultaneously. Both locality and velocity are constantly changing in any measure of time with a large measure of unpredictability. The commodity that we use and refer to as time is examined in detail in a subsequent chapter.

We are superstring energy beings in an energized universe and quite possibly, like all other matter, we are made from star dust. According to the Jefferson Lab in Newport News, Virginia, there are 7×10^{27} energy atoms in the average 150-pound human body. There is 99 percent more space than matter in an atom. It has been calculated that if all of the space in all of the atoms of all of the earth's people was removed, the total compressed atoms of the world's population would be the size of a sugar cube.

Science has further demonstrated that energy is often transferred and changed into new forms and through form, but never lost. Many people have studied and have come to believe in the theory of materialism. Materialism posits that physical matter is the only reality and that everything—including human thought, feeling, and will—can be explained in terms of matter and physical phenomena. Is our consciousness outside of the realm of materialism? Imagine the many discussions and exchanges that must go on relative to twenty-first-century theories.

This is what I refer to as the *quantum consciousness* that facilitates our life-long journey. Our reality is a quantum reality powered by the force of beliefs and dominant thoughts. The creative energy force of our thoughts provides the resonance and molecular movement to construct or change matter. It is a magical way in which the creative universe responds to our requests and many of us have unknowingly taken this for granted for many years. For instance, I have always thought and believed that I have lived a charmed life because everything has usually gone my way. Is this true? Or is it a matter of coincidence? I have often believed that I am incredibly lucky and that I must be doing things correctly. Well, I have done the right things, but I didn't realize it at that time. I was happily attracting those events and experiences that I had thought about and had asked for. Furthermore, I did not know or realize then that I was actually changing my beliefs and the cells in my body and the energies of both. Of course, coincidence, or synchronicity was also involved. I have told my beautiful wife that I have been in love with her all of my life but that I did not know where to find her until I was forty-two years old. My dominant thoughts and beliefs were destined to become a reality, and my long search was made manifest. Both love and fear are very powerful creative forces and our experienced emotions of happiness, peace, beauty, and joy are contagious.

It is the continuous ebb and flow of the energy in the universe that provides synchronicity, according to the Universal Laws. The unexpected and unique events that we so often experience and refer to as coincidental are the synchronicity of our universe. Usually, coincidences are experienced as incredible happenings against all odds, and occurring with exquisite timing. Do you really think that it is a coincidence that you are reading this book? It is synchronicity that provides the manifestation and delivery of those things that we have requested of the universe. Coincidence plays such an important role in our lives, and yet many people do not understand the phenomenon of coincidence. Some people say that there is no such thing as coincidence because all events in our lives are preordained and are necessary for the overall integration of our affairs. Nevertheless, these events must still coincide, or dovetail together and they are entangled in a dynamic tapestry.

Like coincidences, miracles also appear to be a divine intervention. The question is this: By whom? Actually, it is we humans who have unknowingly caused the seeming miracles to happen. Miracles appear to be miracles only because we could not or did not believe that they would occur because of our lack of the knowledge of their causes. Change your beliefs, and watch what happens. Our fervent requests become prayers that manifest a miraculous experience. Learn to see the beauty in synchronicity and in the exquisite timing of the many events interwoven into our lives. Synchronicity is also a central aspect of the Law of Cause and Effect and the Law of Attraction as we shall see in subsequent chapters. Because of science, we now know that our universe is not linear but relational. Once we can recognize the manner in which synchronicity prevails, we can then align our minds and our daily activities to coincide with the universal flow of energy and events. In the 1960s, a popular expression was "go with the flow." This saying holds true today as well. Once we are aware of the process, synchronicity has a marvelous way of providing ever-increasing coincidences; the more we recognize the synchronicity, the more often coincidences occur.

We did not come from anywhere, and we do not go anywhere upon our physical deaths. When the physical body dies, our consciousness simply enters another realm of awareness in another ethereal body. Some religions refer to this phenomenon as life eternal or life everlasting. Consciousness knows neither beginning nor end. As pure consciousness we have always been here in the universe without the man-made concepts of time and space of our earthly virtual realm. In the nonlocal universe, there is nowhere to go. Our permanent, energetic bodies enter and leave from the temporary, physical bodies that we occupy on earth. Other writers often refer to our physical bodies as earth-bodies. Furthermore, our consciousness—or our higher self—does not reside within our human, earth-bodies but projects itself through our physical and mental personality bodies.

There are persons known as mediums who have discovered their unique ability to receive messages from souls after their having departed our physical world. After leaving the physical realm, those soul entities do not go to a distant world but move on to an invisible dimension that circumscribes our realm. Through these mediums, messages are received that suggest that those departed people are watching us, and they hear and know our silent thoughts and energies via telepathic means. It seems to me that we can communicate with physically deceased persons even if we do not always receive a verbal response. This gives new meaning to the question of what we do when we think that no one is watching!

In his 1990 book, *Closer to the Light*, author Melvin L. Morse details numerous examples of near-death experiences wherein people have glimpsed another after-life dimension or reality having left our physical realm. One example describes how a boy born blind returned from a near-death experience. Still blind, he then described in heightened detail, the physical attributes of the physical world that he observed from the after-life realm. What these people observed in the after-life realm often depended upon their perception, imagination, and expectations. Most people met with or observed deceased relatives and many experienced very bright white lights and religious figures. The majority of cases reported upon were described as serenely peaceful and comforting.

Nothing in modern physics will explain how our brain's molecules create consciousness. It is our thoughts, words, and actions that are creative energies. Furthermore, the sciences will never explain how our consciousness came from matter. The reverse is true! Our human consciousness and the conscious universe are the principle driving forces of creation. It is only in the last decade that consciousness has been considered by the scientific community to be a part of the cosmos. Human life and human consciousness are essential to understanding the very nature of our universe. Our reality demands consciousness—much like our senses of touch, taste, smell, and sight require the appropriate organs and features in order to recognize that which is sensed in creation. All of our sensed physical reality exists only in our brain matter. That which we think of as being *out there* externally, is actually occurring in our minds. We use our developed five bodily senses to experience creation, which is our reality. Our projected world is really a Technicolor illusion. The human brain cannot observe anything external to the cranium. Thus, the mind creates and drives our observed realities. Stop, and consider for a moment how we go to sleep and create a dream, a seeming reality complete with other people, animals, emotions, and environments all inside of our heads. We do it all with our eyes closed. We make the same kind of creations in our wakeful state and then project them outward as our realities. We then experience our creation through our five senses.

Many people will have a difficult time believing this, but it is none-the-less true. For many years, we have been incorrectly told that our observed physical reality has been taken inward through our five senses to be imprinted at the back of our eyes and then deciphered and filtered by the brain. It is the human brain that processes a computational model from the billions of bits of information per second to create our so-called observed external virtual reality. For centuries, the Hindu word maya has been used to describe that which is not— or what is called a cosmic illusion of the material world.

Quantum physics has all but destroyed that which we have previously experienced as reality. Quantum theory states that all objects have a dual particle and wave energy nature. An object's behavior exists only as a possibility as wave energy in nature. The same object assumes a particle nature or place and motion only after its wave function collapses. Matter is formed by particle energy called fermions. Experiments have demonstrated that the human mind, with thought energy, can cause the wave function to collapse and cause the particle object to then appear. Quantum waves are possibilities awaiting a change in energy. Stated another way, the particle objects have no real existence or position in space until they are observed or thought about. Without consciousness, matter exists in an undetermined state of probability. The collapse of the wave function is a personal, subjective experience that occurs only within our heads. The same phenomenon may also occur in someone else's head, and that individual will unknowingly believe that he or she had experienced an objective experience.

Our reality and our resonant connection to the cosmos are undeniable to some sciences. The notable scientist Albert Einstein found that a lab experiment could be altered by the concentrated energy of the lab observer's thoughts and eyes. This is called *the observer effect*. The Japanese scientist Dr. Masaru Emoto made a similar discovery in 1999. Experimenting with human thought energies, Dr. Emoto found that when distilled water samples were exposed to loving thoughts and words, the molecular composition of the water changed to brilliant, complex, and colorful snowflake patterns. In contrast, water exposed to negative energy thoughts formed incomplete, asymmetrical patterns with dull colors. Dr. Emoto detailed his experiments in his 2001 book, *The Hidden Messages in Water*. This research created a new awareness of how we can choose to impact not only our own bodies that are comprised of more than 80 percent water but also other individuals and our earth. Objectivity is not possible when the human mind intrudes upon and alters even the most scientific experiments. The observer now becomes the participator, and the universe can never remain the same thereafter. The same energies and governing Universal Laws make the observer into the participant and creator. To this day, I am cognizant of my thoughts when I observe plants, animals, and other humans because of the energies present in thoughts—directed or otherwise!

The observer effect was part of Albert Einstein's theory of relativity. Particles and wave matter electrons are dependent upon probability. We now know that where attention goes, energy flows. Our eyes have the ability to direct our thought energies. Likewise, our intentional thoughts are energies—readily sensed by others who are sensitive enough to do so. On numerous occasions, I have thought about taking a specific action. My wife then verbalized the same thoughts within minutes after my initial thoughts. Like many others, we simply smile and say, "Great minds think alike." Perhaps, the stranger who returns our smile has sensed our friendly, intentional thought as a greeting. Certainly, you can recall having instantly liked someone upon meeting that person for the first time. Do you remember what it was that made you feel that way? Science and psychology have demonstrated that we form our first impressions of others within the first nine seconds of having met them.

Perhaps the same may be said of love at first sight. In a nanosecond, our powerful emotions can become more than an opinion, and then a belief is formed. We can instantly believe that we are in love. Sometimes, our thought energy exchanges can be so powerful and intense that many people cannot tolerate or handle the exchange without feeling unsettled or nervous. In physics, the stronger, higher vibratory energies attract, entrain, and raise the lower energies. There is an awesome power in thought energy.

Happy, loving partnerships with our closest family members and friends provide substantive and very deep relationships in creation. As people begin to evolve and attain a higher awareness and consciousness, they begin to associate with like-minded people to share experiences, techniques, resources, and a special bond. People with happy, higher energy frequencies entrain and attract others to their growing communities. An example is that of the powerful energy created between individuals participating in a passionate kiss, and this subjective experience is called a *qualia*. The intimacy and sexual excitement of lovemaking is also an intense source of energy. Laughter, smiles and hugs, are exchanges of interactive personal energies.

Perhaps you can recall some stories and experiences of animals changing the lives of people exposed to them in nursing homes and private homes. Animals are also energy bodies manifest with earthly roles to play in creation. Many animals can and will express their emotions; however, most humans will not understand animal communications. Without words, an animal is capable of giving and receiving unconditionally, both positive and negative energies with humans.

Electromagnetic and other vibratory forces move and hold electrons and protons together in resonance and atoms combine to form molecules and particle matter. Even our body's cells combine to form cellular communities for strength as body organs. In the atomic field of electromagnetic energies, opposites attract. Our bodies too, are comprised of electrically charged particles in balance with the opposing electromagnetic earth fields. Our thoughts, however, become energy forms at a subatomic string level. The sciences of theoretical physics and quantum mechanics have explored the sublevel of quarks and energies in electromagnetic and super-string theories. At this level, energies do not attract opposites but, instead, attract the same and similar resonant energies.

Quantum physics and the string theory have now shown us that the zero-point field, or ether, is a vast ocean of microscopic vibrations in the space between spinning energies. This space between waves and particles of visible matter is pure energy called dark energy and dark matter and are sometimes denser than the matter. All visible matter in our universe comprises 4.9 percent of the cosmos while the remaining 95 percent is comprised of dark something called dark energy and dark matter. Because dark matter is the opposite of visible matter, it is believed that dark matter must be slightly less than the 5.9 percent of visible matter in order for physical matter to exist. At this time, very little is known about dark energy, but it is believed to possibly consist of weak, interacting particles necessary for the instantaneous transmission of other energy forms. Dark energy is a measurable energy field and has been shown to be the force causing cosmic acceleration and expansion of our universe.

All energy exists in a static state until disturbed or changed by us and then energy changes to real particle matter or reverts back to pure energy. It is our consciousness and intent that create our world. Because consciousness is preeminent, physical objects and events are caused or created by consciousness. Objects and events are only possibilities for our actionable consciousness. In her 2002 book, *The Field: The Quest for the Secret Force of the Universe,* author Lynne McTaggart wrote, "Reality exists then, on a need-to-exist basis. Tomorrow's reality can be ours as a determined need-to-exist basis!" In short, consciousness is primary; the basis of all being and our physical, emotional, and mental realities are the result of our consciousness, our awareness, and our limitless choices. In 2009, Dr. Robert Lanza, MD, wrote in

Biocentrism: How Life and Consciousness are the Keys to Understanding the True Nature of the Universe, "Life and biology are central to being, reality, and the cosmos. Life creates the universe rather than the other way around." Consciousness creates life, and life creates matter in time and space. Take away matter, time, and space, and a silent consciousness remains.

Stop for a moment to consider a few basic facts related to our biology. Until recently, the Darwinian Theory prevailed in science—the theory that proclaimed that our genes determine our lives and our destinies. This belief also fit nicely with scientific materialism. However, our inherited genes are only a part of our cells. Research now shows that each of the body's seventy trillion cells has intelligence and memory. These cells communicate with one another and respond to external and environmental stimulation. For example, our bodies are listening and responding to our minds. These trillions of body cells communicate with our hearts' electrical fields as well. Our emotions and feelings can often become a problem when they are not well understood and controlled. Our feelings are a normal part of physiology, but as energies, feelings are created only by us and not by others. Other people, happenings, or circumstances may trigger our emotions, but our feelings are of our own creation. Why then would we let others rent that space in our heads? Those strong, negative emotions will often give rise to unsocial behaviors and negative opinions that may prevail until they become beliefs. Our feelings can be a very positive force for creativity, and because our feelings are our created energies, we can also change them. It is our core beliefs, which are often subconscious, that prompt our emotions, and conversely, our emotions often form the basis of our beliefs.

Each of the body's seventy trillion cells has receptors to acquire instructions for activity. Our cells also contain our DNA, RNA, our genes, and nucleic acids within the cellular membrane wall. Unless damaged, our inherited DNA cannot be changed, but our genetic memory and genetic activity may be changed with methylation.

According to Dr. Dean Ornish, MD, our genes are predisposed to certain activities or gene expression. However, if we change our thoughts and our lifestyles, we will also change our genetic expression. We can erase and reprogram our genetic memory. The body's seventy trillion cells respond to our subconscious and conscious beliefs as well as our thoughts. Our cells, tissues, and organs respond to stimuli without regard to positive or negative signals. Why not think happy—live happy?

The mind is a powerful and useful creative force for accomplishing many constructive things. If we change our beliefs, we will change our thoughts. When we change our thoughts, we change our actions, habits, biology, and destiny. Leaving anything go to be decided by its self is life by default. We can do all of this by using our minds without succumbing to the belief that we are identified by our minds. The human mind is a tool while the heart is true. We are what we are—consciousness. With infinite possibilities, quantum mechanics enlarges our capacity to reason and to use our imagination in unexpected ways. Quantum mechanics may likely prove to be a better model for understanding human behavior than the classical logic and reasoning.

Our universe is comprised entirely of energy, but surprisingly, only 5 percent of it is materialized as physical matter. In recent months, some members of the scientific community have come to include human consciousness as an important and integral aspect of not only physics, philosophy, religion, and medicine but also cosmology. A universe with consciousness, energy, matter, and intelligence is now talked about in private, but few scientists will publicly acknowledge what they cannot yet measure and demonstrate. For people unfamiliar with these matters related to consciousness, it would be difficult to understand that their favorite easy chair is a creation of multiple energy events of their own making. The easy chair can disappear when they turn off the lights and leave the room. This unpredictability of quantum wave physics and particle physics is addressed in subsequent chapters. Scientists will not likely prove to be the messengers of a shift in global consciousness, but they may eventually document and reinforce the increased knowledge in this realm.

Quantum mechanics may determine who we are and our behaviors, but our thoughts, actions, and behaviors are not without consequence. Let's take a look at the cause and effect of our countless choices in life.

> *The greatest challenge in life is discovering who you are,*
> *the second greatest is being happy with what you find.*
>
> —UNKNOWN

III

Life Is About Choices

With our beliefs and thoughts, we form behavioral choices, and by our choices, we create our reality. Hopefully, with happy hearts and intention we will use the power and the choice to exercise our capacities to create our earthly existences and add meaning to our lives. Far too many people search for meaning in their lives without knowing or realizing that they are looking for themselves. Because we create our virtual reality, we won't find meaning externally, but we can provide meaning to our lives. A happy meaningful life is one wherein we become more conscious and loving human beings.

A life's purpose is entirely another matter. It is with our human volition and intention that we make choices. Our choices are made through our creative intentions. With our intentions, every decision that we make causes something to happen. A different decision causes something entirely different to occur. Because free will or volition is part of our psyche, we have the capability to make choices and to enjoy our creative endeavors and reality. Who do you believe you are? Once we uncover and know who we are, with our capabilities to create our reality, we will have intentional choices to make. Our reality has always been and will continue to be available at four basic levels. Reality is simply the experience of one or more of the levels created by the human mind. The human experiences of reality range from illusion and fantasy to self-actualization in total consciousness, or God consciousness. The choice is ours. If we think of something and believe it, we can make nearly anything happen.

Twenty million bits of data per second are processed by our subconscious minds automatically and forty bits per second are processed by our conscious minds. The enormous capacity of the human brain is difficult to describe. The human brain requires this incredible neural capacity in order to interpret and process the information required for both our conscious choices and the subconscious roots for our choices. Recall that our virtual reality is determined by our dominant thoughts and beliefs—whether conscious or otherwise. To raise our levels of consciousness, we only have to use critical thinking and reasoning to make informed choices with corresponding consequences.

In chapter seven, the philosopher Plato's four levels of reality are described in detail. Of Plato's observed levels of reality, the level of the experience of bodily senses can be sensually self-indulgent and pleasurable without regard to human virtue. In contrast, eudaimonism focuses on meaning and self-realization and defines human well-being in terms of the degree to which a human is functioning with virtue and the gene expression of good health. Eudaimonism is also devoid of the stress from the disappointments caused by failed hedonistic expectations. According to the ancient philosopher Aristotle, a basic hedonistic lifestyle is the pursuit of pleasure as the primary intrinsic good while avoiding pain.

Stop and think about the many conscious choices that we make in a single day. Consider the consequences of those choices. It's safe to say that some of our choices did not work out for the best. We should take responsibility for unwanted choices and remain happy with the knowledge that we can create more options and choices. Our lives are a continuous series or chain of choices in our wakeful states of being. Knowingly or otherwise, we design our lives and our evolving realities with our thoughts and our choices. If we change one brief thought, we will change your entire chain of thought and subsequent experiences. We are better served with deliberate, intentional thought processes and decisions as opposed to facing life with a random, coasting result. Both our casual and our intentional thoughts are energies that will attract events to our lives and determine our realities. Our thoughts are our future realities, and our thoughts are largely influenced by our conscious and subconscious beliefs.

Our casual, daily thoughts are equally as powerful as our intentional, concentrated, and deliberate thoughts. Incredible as it sounds, all of our thoughts are energy forms that attract our life events. We have accumulated beliefs that are stored and programmed at two levels of our awareness—our wakeful consciousness and our larger, subconscious collection of filtered beliefs. In his 1988 piece *Knowledge Systems, Inc.*, Willis Harmon wrote: "A person's total belief system is an organization of beliefs and expectancies that the person accepts as true of the world he or she lives in, verbal and nonverbal, implicit and explicit, conscious and unconscious." How many of us truly know who we are in that we have the capacity to create our own realities and destinies? We shall see in subsequent chapters that there is nothing random or coincidental in our balanced universe. We think therefore it is! We are responsible for our unique and interwoven realities. Our beliefs generate our experiences. Happy, relaxed attitudes and beliefs create happy life experiences. That is why we are here on earth.

The choices that we make are nearly always influenced by our life principles. We all have many life principles—whether we are consciously aware of them or not. These life principles are formed from our foundation of beliefs. There will always be a single, dominant principle guiding our thoughts, choices, and behaviors. Our life principles may change and may also cease as we evolve in awareness and self-actualization. Character is not something we were born with, but character is developed by our choices in life. Have you thought about your life principles or defined them? I invite you to first stop and recall other people with very obvious life principles. Here are some examples of lives with obvious principles: a life of power and subjugation; a life of passivity and service with self-depreciation; a life of safety and security; a life of duty and compliance; a life of monetary wealth, success, recognition, and approval; a life of excitement and adventure; and perhaps a happy life of unconditional love and totality of consciousness. Our accumulated beliefs will often determine our basic life principles. A life principle is a generalized intention or purpose that is applied to a person's daily choices and circumstances. Our choices, when made based upon our beliefs and our principles, will determine the purpose of our lives. These choices are another perspective on creating our reality. A very large majority of the people in this country have never thought about their life principles or defined them. Living a life of default, these people will continue to live on autopilot with only reactionary responses to events in their lives. To discover and know our dominant principles, we need only look to Herbert Maslow's book, *Human Hierarchy of Needs*. This book will help us to consider what is of importance and value in our lives. With knowledge, we can change our creative beliefs and our lives.

In a world faced with growing problems in nearly every facet of daily life, more and more people are searching for a meaningful purpose and happiness in their lives. Perhaps it is our higher selves that are restless and in pursuit of change. At some point in our lives, we will eventually conclude that there must be something more and something better for our continued lives. A sense of something missing or a longing can be the beginning of the discovery of our true meanings and purposes in life. The extent to which we can intentionally create our realities will depend upon our level of awareness and our commitment to making the right choices throughout our lives. When we are sincere in our commitments, synchronicity will bring to us the opportunities and the necessary resources.

Our universe is in constant evolution, and so it is with the human condition. There are now numerous books and other resources available about living a life of intention, about living deliberately with purpose, and about many other approaches to personal growth and transformation. There also appears to be evidence of a change in our planet's spiritual axis. Many of the centuries-old spiritual traditions and beliefs of East Asia and India are now being embraced by people with an awakening consciousness and transformation in the United States. At the same time, many developing Asian and Middle Eastern countries are exchanging their ancient beliefs to embrace the capitalistic and monetary creed of modern Europe and North America. Coupled with the earth's changing spiritual axis, advances in technology and communications now demand and promote our evolutionary transformation. These are exciting but troubling times, and we are at an evolutionary milestone. While the world is constantly changing, we must decide whether we wish to simply observe reality or create our reality and destiny? To create change, it is imperative that we first know our capabilities and who we are.

Before reading any further, take a moment to determine if you know your true inner being that I am referring to. The process is really quite simple. Close your eyes if necessary, and place your attention on the constant stream of words that you hear inside of your head. This is the voice of your ego, a necessary aspect and functioning of your mind. Even your attention is a function of the mind. But the real you is the silent listener who hears these words. When our physical, earthly bodies die, and when our minds are also gone, our consciousness will live on! Both the physical body and the human mind are like a jacket and covering for the consciousness. Consciousness is awareness without thought. It becomes critically important to know the difference between the awareness of our thoughts and the silent awareness that requires no thought.

In his book, *Do No Harm: Stories of Life, Death, and Brain Surgery*, British neurosurgeon Henry Marsh, MD, wrote that what we often believe to be real is actually an illusion. He used pain as an example. For instance, when we feel pain in our hands, it is not actually in our hands at all; the pain is in our brains. Our brains create a three-dimensional model of the world. The brain then associates the nerve impulses coming from the pain receptors in the hand with pain in the hand, and then the brain creates the illusion that the hand is in pain. Without our creative brains, we would feel or sense no pain. Dr. Marsh reports that our bodies generate electricity, and this allows our nervous system to send signals to our brains. These signals are actually electrical charges delivered from cell to cell and create nearly instantaneous communication.

Dr. Marsh further describes how our thoughts are also electric-chemistry, but the sciences do not yet fully understand all of the complexities of the functions of the human brain. He reports that if we don't have a conventional religious belief system, then our thinking about our consciousness and the universe connection is a substitute or compensation of sorts for religion. Our human brains contain billions of neurons. No one knows exactly how many, but it is believed to be approximately eighty-six billion neurons. In comparison, there are thought to be two hundred to four hundred billion stars in just the Milky Way. Half of these brain neurons are located in our cerebellum, which is about half the volume of our entire central nervous system. These neurons interact and form trillions of connections in the brain and produce personality, memory, intelligence, and dream sequencing. Then our brain cells shrink by about 60 percent to allow for efficient waste removal and detoxification while we sleep. It has been formerly believed that we were born with a certain number of brain cells and that this number was static throughout our lives. Science now knows that the brain has neuroplasticity and neurogenesis—which is the capacity to regrow, reshape, reform, and reorganize neural pathways and connections for functional communications. For many years, we were thought to be using but a very small percentage of our large human brain capacity. Now, it is known and documented that we are and have been unknowingly using a large percentage of the brain's capacity to process the millions of pieces of information per second in our daily routines of reality.

So who do you think you are? Your purpose for existence on this planet is to discover your true identity and with human awareness and consciousness, to create your reality and happily enjoy your multidimensional creation. It is through the human experience that we are destined to create, to express ourselves, and to experience our creation. The grand universal scheme does not require or demand anything of us but provides for our evolutionary growth. Consciousness is awareness without thought. When we become conscious of the difference between our thinking and our awareness, it is called an awakening of awareness. Unfortunately, not every person can or will find his or her true self or an awakening. There are, of course, those people who are not the least bit interested in a personal growth of awareness and consciousness. Others will seek enlightening but never experience it. As reported earlier, our beliefs generate our experiences. Any limiting beliefs can also impair our capacity to change our realities and experiences. If we think or believe that we can't, then we won't! There are many others who will not explore and discover their true selves and purposes. Perhaps they are fearful of any change that will expose them to a new world of ideas and new struggles. Perhaps they should consider that "I can" is better than IQ.

Obviously, each of us has a different script to follow with changing beliefs and perspectives. There are many others who will continue to placate or pacify their long-held, unfounded and harmful beliefs. They will see only what they wish to see for whatever reasons. They will be left behind in the rapidly evolving theater of our reality.

Our long-held deepest core beliefs are the most difficult to change. To change a belief that is no longer appropriate or useful, we must step out of our comfort zone and examine that belief, how we acquired it, and our consequent behaviors. We must be consciously aware of our beliefs and their impact upon our emotions, behaviors, and lives. The easiest way to displace an unwanted belief is to replace it with new information. We must simply choose a new or revised belief and continue to consciously follow it as a habit until it becomes imbedded in the subconscious as well. It also helps to trust and believe in the process to facilitate the creating of ourselves.

There are many more people seeking enlightenment—believing it to be enlightenment of the mind—to find wisdom and purpose in their lives. Actually, the purpose of our human experience is to find our true inner identity, to create our reality, and to enjoy our human experience. The personal enlightening that I describe is not necessarily spiritual, and it is much more than the wisdom of a gathered knowledge. Accumulated knowledge would be best used to better our lives and the lives of others. Those persons seeking enlightenment may eventually find that enlightenment is actually a continuous process of incremental *enlightening* rather than an end goal. In the ageless competition between the sciences and the humanities, the humanities will study the meaning of the human experience, while the sciences will bring new ideas, growth, and technological advances to society. Science and the humanities are not mutually exclusive.

Science, technology, and the Internet are profoundly changing our societal and institutional beliefs as well as prompting evolutionary change. We are all interconnected and are a universal community when we view the many crises as global. As more and more people come to experience a new awareness and consciousness, our planet will evolve because of the critical mass gathered. Each of us will choose a separate and unique path by the choices that we will make. For many of us, the path has begun with studying, learning, and looking for answers to our many questions. We have found that information, knowledge, and education are entirely separate and not always progressively experienced. Moreover, an accumulated knowledge and personal experience should be made actionable in our lives and the lives of others. Some people have sought change by pursuing a scientific approach and have discovered an awareness that does not depend entirely upon an expanded knowledge. The sciences can be very helpful for our understanding of the processes in life.

The human body and consciousness are both a wondrous marvel in so many aspects. The brain comprises 2 percent of the body's weight, yet it consumes 20 percent of the body's energy even at rest.

Science has determined that the conscious mind is capable of receiving approximately forty bits of information per second. The subconscious mind can receive and store more than twenty million bits of data per second. We will not even be aware that the information or perceived ideas are then programmed into our subconscious mind, and this information then forms elements of our beliefs. It is important to know that most people are totally unaware of the fact that 95 percent of their decisions, actions, emotions, and behaviors come from their subconscious minds because of their beliefs, according to Marianne Szegedy-Maszak in her 2005 article "Mysteries of the Mind: Your Unconscious Is Making Your Everyday Decisions," in *U.S. News & World Report.* Most of us have been operating, functioning on a daily basis without an awareness of why we are doing so, based on countless subconscious, programmed beliefs. We are conscious of only a fraction of our beliefs until we choose to examine those beliefs that are hidden from our awareness. Perhaps it's time for a reality check.

A happy life of intent and choice is a life of conscious action. A life lived by chance is a life lived in unconscious reaction. Ask yourself this: Are you a bystander, watching your life unfold in a random fashion. Are you reactive instead of proactive? Do you recognize your thoughts and know your beliefs and your intentions in order to create and enjoy your reality and your tomorrow? Understand that nothing is random in life. Everything has a time and purpose. Our lives are a continuous series of possibilities, opportunities, and choices with significant consequences. Consider the many choices that you make in a single day. Do you realize that your thoughts and actions often have an immediate consequence? The thoughts, choices that we make daily and their consequences are readily apparent once we become aware of them. Our deep, subconscious beliefs are also prompting our conscious thoughts and influencing our actions and our choices in life. Some of these deep, subconscious beliefs are not only false, but they may also be destructive and dysfunctional.

These undesirable beliefs that are causing unwanted behaviors can be changed once identified.

Seventy percent of our thoughts are negative and redundant, according to Daniel Coleman and Greg Braden in their book *Measuring the Immeasurable: The Scientific Case for Spirituality.* Our subconscious beliefs have been formed and collected for many years and even over several lifetimes. The words of our parents, teachers, friends, and politicians as well as, events, and other environmental factors have influenced and structured our collective beliefs. From infancy onward, we are told how to behave, how to act according to others' beliefs, and even how to think. Once developed, our beliefs became a filter through which we perceive our present realities and create our futures. How we see ourselves and recognize our capabilities are also defined by our beliefs. Both our conscious and subconscious beliefs influence everything in our realities, oftentimes with very powerful emotions. Both our conscious and subconscious beliefs can influence our bodies and our health. Our beliefs can even influence the physical properties and matter in the universe. Our beliefs are creative forces and will not only generate our experiences but also the evolutionary process.

The energy of our subconscious beliefs is often loaded with stored emotion. The stronger of these emotions are the natural ones of happiness, joy, love, and fear. Interestingly, our thoughts do not always provoke our actions, but our emotions nearly always promote actions, even if we are only thinking about an unsettling emotion or trying to change our thinking. Strong emotions can rapidly become our opinions and can continue to form or change our beliefs. The reverse may also occur when our hidden, subconscious beliefs as well as our conscious beliefs become the roots of our opinions and behaviors. Our subconscious beliefs and programming can also unconsciously hijack our best intentions. We need not be destined to repeat our mistakes and sufferings or to slow our evolutionary progress. We have a choice for tomorrow. Why wait for repeated, unwanted experiences to be brought to our awareness when we can instead prompt new and rewarding life experiences?

Any single belief represents one of many quantum possibilities. When we can see the limitless possibilities available, we can then change our perceptions, beliefs, thoughts, and experiences. To change our experience is to create our own unique reality. When we change, the world around us will change. Consider that the subconscious retentions of our prior experiences and habits are the basis of our actions today. Author Robert M. Williams in his 2004 book, *PSYCH-K: The Missing Peace in Your Life*, wrote, "There are many programs available to discover or expose the many unknown subconscious beliefs that we have formed. If we bring these beliefs into our conscious awareness for examination, we can dispel the energy of these unwanted beliefs, rewrite our genetic software, and transform our entire belief filtering system." When we reverse and change our filtering system, we can then direct our biology and our destiny. Without professional assistance, we may never know many of our subconscious beliefs that are influencing and directing our actions and decisions and even the very manner in which we filter new information. Numerous new programs offer lists of specific questions for us to ask ourselves and check our true, subconscious, and hidden beliefs with simple kinesiology muscle testing.

Much like our thoughts, our beliefs reverberate with an energy that also impacts both our emotions and our health. Our human consciousness is awareness without thought, and it is the human consciousness that powers both our bodies and our minds. Consider that human consciousness is much like a ball of energy dropped into a human fetus prior to birth at quickening. Occurring during pregnancy, quickening is believed to be the first movements and signs of life. It is then easier to understand that we should welcome and embrace the higher vibratory energies of positive thoughts and beliefs. It is the developing human mind that creates the phonetic voice to the thoughts for the listening energy body of consciousness. After a time of growth and experience, the human mind also develops volition and intention.

There are many people who believe that we have little or no choice or free will and that human volition is but a false definition of part of our mental function. It is also believed by some that everything in our human existence has been predetermined and that we therefore have no free will or choice. The truth of the matter is that every aspect of our lives has been predetermined at a higher level of consciousness and creation. Remember that nothing is random or without purpose. Because our existence and our awareness are trapped in the lower level of the physical and emotional realm, we appear to have the capability of free will or volition. So while we are operating in this physical world that we have created, we can use our free will and change our lives. This too was preordained. We have free will, and we have choices to make based upon our levels of awareness and consciousness.

In our Western world, we are intellectually biased, and many will find it difficult to find the necessary balance between our ego, intellect, and spirit. It is our volition—or will—that is the impetus for all of our creative thoughts and actions.

In the seventeenth century, the French philosopher Rene Descartes altered history when he developed a theory that earned him this title: "Father of Modern Philosophy." The Cartesian theory of dualism posits that the mind and body are totally separate entities and acknowledges the human awareness and consciousness as a product of the mind. Consciousness would then terminate with the death of the body and the cessation of the mind. Descartes has been remembered throughout the ages because he declared this: "Cogito ergo sum." This phrase means "I think, therefore I am." Rene Descartes was a brilliant philosopher, lawyer, and scientist of the time. There is a contemporary joke about Descartes walking into a bar where the waitress asks him this: "Would you like some wine?" Descartes replies, "I think not," and promptly disappears.

It would now seem that Descartes was probably unaware of the relationship of our energy bodies to the unified field. We now know that our consciousness is primary and causal to our reality. Our physical reality does not create our consciousness. It is our consciousness that defines our physical existence and our reality. For centuries, we have been made to believe that our physical evolution is primary and causal to our consciousness. Both religion and science have delayed our recognition of our conscious being. But things are now changing rapidly! If Rene Descartes were alive today, he would likely say "I think; therefore, it is."

> *We are part of this universe; we are in this universe, but perhaps more important than both of those facts, is that the universe is in us.*
>
> —Neil deGrasse Tyson

IV

Our Beliefs Create Reality

Far too long there has been confrontation and conflict because of our emotional differences, our acquired beliefs, and our unique opinions. It is not the nature of our inherent divinity to be so limited by our mental-emotional differences. The nature of our realities, our existence, and our consciousness has intrigued the human race for thousands of years. Since the earliest centuries, the related studies of philosophy, metaphysics, ontology, and spirituality have evolved and have complemented one another. One only has to look at the state of affairs in our current world to see the conflict of beliefs regarding politics, religion, and social issues—such as wealth distribution, gun control, cultural practices, education, and many more contemporary crises. It would seem that our mental constructs and resulting chaos have preceded a naturally happy, loving disposition.

Our beliefs have often been incorrectly thought to be the same as our opinions. Our opinions are a product of our wakeful, conscious minds, and our basic beliefs reside in our subconscious minds until brought forward to our wakeful, conscious minds. Our beliefs can influence our opinions, and conversely, our opinions may become our beliefs when they are experienced repeatedly. Both our opinions and our beliefs are flexible and changing and are not always in accord with the perceptions and beliefs of countless others. Our beliefs will often form the roots of both our intentions and our behaviors—which is a perfect environment for conflict.

Our beliefs are formed through a structured process in which we observe and evaluate everything in our lives. We interpret the world around us according to our conscious and subconscious beliefs. These beliefs are formed and changed by our experiences and observations. Our beliefs often become a combination of logic and emotions—of both the heart and mind. Remember too, that our bio-electromagnetic bodies may be crippled and diseased by our powerfully creative and destructive thoughts, beliefs, and emotions. Too often our beliefs are reduced to a fundamental judgment of what is right, wrong, and inappropriate. After many years, some of our beliefs are outlived and are no longer relevant. In order for us to continue to evolve, we should perhaps periodically examine our basic beliefs and review their usefulness in creating our reality. Why not look to happy, positive thoughts and beliefs?

Restrictive and unnecessary beliefs will keep many people from knowing and experiencing a meaningful, happy life. Hopefully, many will come to realize that our individual belief systems should include the knowledge that our dominant thoughts and beliefs will create our life experiences, our realities. The act of believing is the engine of our evolutionary process because our beliefs prompt our intentions and our actions. Today, science can support both philosophical and religious beliefs because there is a better understanding of the nature of consciousness.

Many people are unaware of the mental, emotional, and physical aspects of their persona and remain ignorant of their higher selves. Step out of your comfort zone for a few minutes and challenge your preconceived beliefs. We should understand just what spirituality means to various people. Spirituality is simply the quality or human state of being spiritual. To be spiritual is to be cognizant of our connection to a higher creative power. Spirituality does not require religion or science, however both will corroborate our beliefs. Spirituality is a very broad term, and its meaning varies with our unique perspectives and beliefs. For many, a spiritual connection comes through nature and the universe. Others consider spirituality to be centered on or concerned with service to others. A very large portion of our population believes that spirituality is something granted to individuals by religion. Our universe is of the ethereal spirit, but spirit does not necessarily imply a sacred or holy dimension. Our innate divinity is the source of our spirituality. Spirituality is what we personally make of it. Spirituality is dependent upon our orientation, awareness, and personal experience. Our human evolution on this earth includes a rich history of study and documentation of the nature of our beliefs.

For centuries, we have pondered reality and the nature of being. Both our realities and our spiritual beliefs are subjective experiences. Metaphysics is a traditional branch of philosophy and is concerned with the fundamental nature of being and the world that encompasses the nature of our being. A central branch of metaphysics is ontology. It was an ancient Greek philosopher Parmenides (540–515 BC) who described ontology as the study of the nature of being, existence, and reality and the basic categories of human beings and their relationships.

The purpose of our human existence involves the inherent awesome power of our human capacity for knowledge and creativity. Once we become aware of these capabilities, we have a choice that should include the freedom of a loving, happy heart and the ultimate totality of consciousness. An open heart will see love in all of creation. We are here in this physical realm on earth to find our true nature of being and to increase human consciousness. Our reality can be better than our dreams.

Our conscious and subconscious beliefs determine 95 percent of our behaviors and quite possibly hold us captive to our unfounded, long-held fears and opinions. Our beliefs may range from the profane to the profound, and beliefs are left to the imagination and knowledge of the experiencer. Strive to be the conscious, happy, and loving observer.

Because our universe requires balance in all things, our conflicting beliefs may cause a temporary psychological distress called *cognitive dissonance*. Quantum physics reflects our awareness and understanding of human consciousness as related to our physical world. Science and quantum physics are rapidly changing how we view both our established beliefs and our reality.

As evolving beings, we come to this physical and mental realm to continue our personal spiritual growth. Reincarnation returns us to the same physical realm repeatedly as we grow from inexperienced infant souls to old, matured, knowledgeable beings. We also evolve and grow in awareness and consciousness. We eventually experience four levels of reality in a progressive manner, and we experience some more rapidly than others. We almost always return to a new human existence within a previous family of relatives and friends in order to experience and learn from lessons lived and shared in a balanced universe.

Our lifelong journey is often described as a path—not entirely unlike the yellow brick road in the movie *The Wizard of Oz*. Our paths are both our personal search for reality and an individual identity and our purpose for existence.

The natural laws of the universe are immutable and provide a balance of equal and opposite consequences for all energies in the cosmos. Our universe is in constant evolution, and so it is with the human condition. There are numerous books about quantum physics, human psychology, esoteric studies, and scientific discoveries that provide us with the knowledge and direct experience of creating our intentional reality. For too long we have been led to believe that our reality is material and objective. As a planetary society, we evolve one person at a time. We each create a growing community, nation, and the world.

Regardless of limiting beliefs, each of us can create our own narrative and act with intention and gratitude. We must examine our conscious beliefs and some of our subconscious beliefs. In 1903, author James Allen wrote in his book *As a Man Thinketh* of the importance of knowing that our dominant thoughts and beliefs create our reality. This is also an important message of this book. Our beliefs and our thoughts contain a very powerful energy, and our beliefs create our biology and our destiny. Why not employ happy, loving beliefs and thoughts? What we have thought about in the past has created our reality today, and what we think about today will determine our future experience. It is important to know too that what we think about and how we think about it is often determined by our unknown and subconscious beliefs.

According to Tuned Body.com, scientists can now show how our dominant thoughts can cause specific molecular changes to our genes. Like a musical instrument, our bodies must be tuned to the vibration of the universe. Our perceptions are reflected in our bodies' chemistry, and our genetic activity may change on a daily basis—involuntarily or through our intentions. Stop, and consider for a moment what a belief is and how our beliefs influence our intentions. The Oxford Dictionary and medical definition of *belief* is "an acceptance, trust, faith, or confidence that something or someone is true or exists." Our conscious beliefs are interrelated with our opinions, viewpoints, impressions, presumptions, assumptions, inferences, and conclusions. Subconscious beliefs are formed from infancy onward through life, and the beliefs sometimes change to rigid beliefs that are based upon our experiences and our emotions. Most subconscious beliefs remain hidden from our awareness, even though they govern and impact 95 percent of our actions, health, and perceptions. It is good to also remember that public opinion is not necessarily synonymous with knowledge. One has to consider that if our dominant beliefs and thoughts are the creative force of our individual reality, why would we choose to wander this planet without knowing that we create our life experiences and how we create that experience?

It is not a coincidence that you are reading this book. You have created the circumstances that brought about this experience. Regardless of our limiting beliefs, each of us can change our reality through intention, and we can know our biology better as well. It begins when we examine our dominant thoughts and discover our subconscious and conscious beliefs. We should take a closer look and examine the elements of human consciousness, the synchronicity of events, and the biological role of our molecular cells. Our raised awareness will include having a direct experience of our self being fully present and knowing our capacity and any limitations. With experiential knowledge, we can form or change our creative dominant beliefs.

We design our journeys with our dominant thoughts and beliefs. It was not by chance that we were placed upon this earth. As cocreators, we are here to create our reality and enjoy the experience. We must take responsibility for our lives and realize that we create our experience as we evolve in consciousness. We are constantly in the process of creating our realities in order to enjoy our respective creations. Every minute of every day, we create manifestation as fast as we can think. Events, circumstances, happenings, conditions, and experiences are all created from consciousness. The creation begins from within our heads. We choose from a multitude of possibilities—both conscious and unconscious possibilities. A new worldview within Newtonian physics now includes an esoteric model of observed reality. Because we actually create our reality and our physical universe, we should first know and understand our true identities and our very powerful capabilities and their consequences.

Our entire planet is experiencing a transformational shift in consciousness. Our very description of humanity is changing rapidly. Quantum physics is now documenting a new paradigm and model that shows that our reality is determined by our consciousness. Because of the chaos and unpredictability of quantum theory, the correlation between consciousness and the Universal Laws of the universe has yet to be documented fully. From the infinite possibilities of lifestyles, our mental intent actualizes our reality. There is an incredible power and energy in our thoughts and beliefs. For many years religion, politics, and government have held us captive to crippling ideologies and beliefs without providing satisfactory answers to our many inquiries. Today, many people are searching externally for meaning and purpose in their lives when they should instead go within for the answers they seek. They also yearn for a change in their lives that will lead to the peaceful resolution of many of the world's global concerns. Millions of people are now aware of the evolutionary leap or advancement that grows larger with each passing day. Our lives and humanity are rapidly changing.

An evolving global enlightenment is facilitated by increasing scientific discoveries and because of expanded digital universal communications. Many people refer to this historic movement as an awakening because of the esoteric nature of our discovery. This movement is not necessarily a religious experience. These evolutionary changes will set the stage for a new and better tomorrow, but we must first come to know ourselves as individuals, much like the Socratic theme of *know thyself*. When we truly know ourselves and our capabilities, we will know the secrets of the universe. Our human physiology is in a constant state of recreating and repairing, and our human awareness and consciousness are also evolving. Our very future is now at stake and will depend upon our individual awareness and that of the larger global community.

At this current time in our evolution, we have reached the point where our enlightened awareness now includes scientific confirmation of the human capability to create our experiences of reality. A new era of quantum physics has brought with it the knowledge that our human consciousness creates our observed reality. The sciences are discovering and documenting how human consciousness is the key to nearly everything in our physical existence and beyond.

Wisdom is the knowledge of truth in an unchanging reality. We are fortunate to live in an age of improved science, medicine, communications, and other resources—such as television, the Internet, books, DVDs, and CDs. We can research and learn from virtually unlimited information about our biology. Tired of being just casual observers living a life of default, many people are now finding the answers to their many questions in their unfulfilled lives. They are discovering their true identities, their core beliefs, and their purposes. In recent years, there has been a substantial increase in the number of available resources that focus directly upon searching the human consciousness. Much like everything else in our instant society, people want it now—immediate answers, knowledge, and enlightenment. Actually, enlightenment comes to us in bits and pieces, and then we come to a sudden awareness of matters that we previously did not fully know or understand. Some people call these aha moments when they experience an epiphany of sorts. A quantum is a small amount of energy emitted as very small packets (the smallest of the small). Our consciousness will expand slowly, in quantum elements. People in the habit of saying, "I can't believe that," will suddenly and intuitively know the truth of things and their beliefs will change.

It is interesting to consider that most of what we imagine and experience in our creative minds exists only in our minds, yet we can still experience it as our reality. Our parent thoughts and beliefs give birth to all things. It is important to remember that what we think about and how we think is often influenced or determined by our subconscious beliefs. Reality begins within our heads; our past and our future are created from a centered position of the present. Our thoughts are linked together from end to end. If we change one link, the change will lead to different thoughts and different results. If we create the chain with intention, we will create our reality and our life with intention. Each and every change of thought sets in motion a change in the cosmos beyond our comprehension. Our creative thoughts are most effective when repeated often. Our casual and daily thoughts are equally as powerful as our intentional, concentrated, and deliberate thoughts. Incredible as it sounds, all of our thoughts are forms of energy that attract and change our lives. We create our actionable reality!

So what are your beliefs, and who do you think you are? You are the most important person you could ever get to know. Take the time to go within to better know yourself and your beliefs. It is then easier to live in your own skin and to be honest in relationships with others. Even more important than discovering your true self is the experience of creating your identity. We can know and define our needs and wants and see that they include the well-being of others. We have accumulated our core beliefs and values that are stored and programmed in two levels of our human awareness. Our beliefs are stored in our wakeful consciousness and our larger subconscious. Biologist Bruce Lipton said in his book *The Biology of Belief* that a person's belief system is an organization of beliefs and expectancies that a person accepts as true of the world he or she lives in—verbal and nonverbal, implicit and explicit, and conscious and unconscious. How many of us know who we are with the capacity to create our own reality with the creative force of our dominant thoughts and beliefs?

Our world changes dramatically when we suddenly discover how synchronicity works with the law of attraction in a manifest reality. We can then see the interconnectedness of all things and events. In the 1939 Warner Bros. movie *The Wizard of Oz* Dorothy and friends looked behind the curtain and found not only the wizard but also a new reality. Would you like to peek behind the curtain to see for yourself a new reality and discover who you really are?

> Wisdom begins with a loving heart.
>
> —UNKNOWN

V

The Happy Universe

The Creator gave us a wondrous universe in perfect balance and order in which we were meant to be happy. There are Universal Laws controlling our physical universe that are recognized by the sciences. These time-tested Universal Laws have been compiled by the sciences in order to understand the silent workings of our universe and the larger cosmos. A happy, open, loving heart will easily function within the Universal Laws. A closer look at some of these natural laws may provide us with an understanding of how our lives are impacted by the functions of our universe. Our knowledge and direct observation of these laws at work will affect our beliefs and resulting realities.

The seven Universal Laws include the following: the Law of Mentality, the Law of Vibration, the Law of Polarity, the Law of Gender, the Law of Rhythm, the Law of Correspondence, and the Law of Cause and Effect. These are the Universal Laws or principles by which everything in the universe is governed. Our universe exists in perfect harmony by virtue of these laws, and consciously or not, we use these laws in our daily lives, often simultaneously. When we are aware of how these laws work synergistically, we are more likely to be happy with their application in our lives.

We create and cause our mental and physical realities from the causal level of consciousness. What is commonly thought of as the law of karma is actually the Universal Law of Cause and Effect. What goes around comes around. The Law of Cause and Effect applies to the three planes of our earthly existence—the mental and physical, the astral, and the causal and universal planes. On the mental and physical plane, our concepts of time and space create a lag in time, a difference between the cause and the eventual effect. With creative intervention in our thoughts and actions, we can manifest that which we wish—first in the causal and universal plane, then the astral plane, and then in the physical and mental world. Of course, there are other circumstances when our unintentional thoughts will create or cause a manifest effect.

Karma is an intrinsic societal component of Buddhism and Hinduism. For centuries, the law of karma has been viewed by both Hindu and Buddhist religions to be the sum of an individual's actions and prior states of existence and has been thought to be decisive of the individual's fate in any future existences. In a way, this is typical and no different from other religious ideologies. Actually, karmic debt is a normal cycle of life with cause and effect, and any debt is strictly a matter of one's belief. The law of karma differs from the original Universal Law of Cause and Effect because the Law of Cause and Effect is without the judgmental aspect of any debt owed. Without a debt owed, there can be no control by religion. If we knowingly create our reality, why would we wish to burden ourselves with the notion of mental karma? We can instead learn to be responsible for the consequences of our creative thoughts and actions. With knowledge, we change our beliefs and our lives.

The Law of Cause and Effect in our universe requires equilibrium and balance in all aspects of a complex system. As humans, we are an integral part of this grand universe, creating a physical and mental reality that must also be in balance with the universal laws. Any perceived luck, chance, or random events and actions in nature are nonexistent in our lives. The societal phenomenon of karma similarly occurs only in the lower realms of consciousness—the physical and mental level and the astral level. In accordance with the Law of Cause and Effect, all events and actions are dependent upon and interwoven with all other events. Cause and effect will necessarily balance the universal energy field. Cause and effect will also demand equity because the effect will always exert its influence back on the cause in the exact proportion that was initially sent, causing an equal and opposite reaction. This is Isaac Newton's third law of motion.

Creation—what could be easier? In his 1995 book *The Way of the Wizard: Twenty Spiritual Lessons for Creating the Life You Want*, writer and teacher Deepak Chopra said, "The most creative act that you will undertake is the act of creating yourself." It is our intention that creates not only our thoughts and actions but our realities as well. Too many people are constantly caught up in right versus wrong. Do we do the right things for the wrong reasons? Or do we do the wrong things for the right reasons? There is no right or wrong of anything unless we think it so. Hence, the expression: "It is what it is." There is no right or wrong of it, but our thoughts and actions have consequences and will demand a balance. We have the choice to have the same experiences repeatedly or to learn and evolve beyond the concept of a karmic cycle. Our goal should be to attempt to avoid creating an imbalance and to eventually rise above the level of cause and effect to the higher levels of consciousness beyond the causal and universal level. Too many people think that they are bound to and influenced by karma at the mental level. If they believe that, then it will be so. They have manifested their own unhappy problem.

The basic Law of Cause and Effect operates at all levels of creation as an energy issue—not only in the realm of physical matter but also in the realm of our thoughts and emotional patterns. The entire universe consists of interrelated planes of physical, emotional, and mental aspects. Note that our thoughts, our words, and our actions and deeds are creative. A causal thought or action may reach out in time as we know it and across lifetimes to bring an equitable effect back to the causal origin or the person who created the circumstances.

The patterns and events of our lives are interwoven with those of countless other lives through synchronicity, and they govern every event in our lives in accordance with the balance of cause and effect. If we think about something, we may as well have done it as far as the universe is concerned. Sometimes, the balancing effect returns to us several times until the lessons are learned, and we can move on. The Law of Cause and Effect includes the closely related Law of Attraction that is discussed in chapter seven. With the Law of Attraction we can learn to summon both positive and negative effects to our lives. Affirmations are a very popular use of the Law of Attraction, and repetitive sayings are used to retrain our brains by habituation and to convince us of positive new beliefs and behaviors. Our lives today are the effect of our dominant, previous thoughts, and our thoughts and intentions today will create our realities of tomorrow. It is important to realize that we can affect the cause, but we cannot change the effect once created. When we wish to change our reality, we must change the causes.

When we observe that the Law of Cause and Effect pertains to all matter and events from the causal level of consciousness to the gross physical and mental plane, we can begin to realize that we can transcend all the unwanted effects created in the lower levels of consciousness. We create our cause and effect realities with our thoughts, beliefs, words, and actions. Our thoughts, words, and actions are all produced by creative energy. Consider for a moment the consequence of our beliefs and dominant thoughts. In each and every nanosecond of our lives, we select or design our immediate future from a multitude of possibilities. With each ever-changing possibility we again unconsciously select and determine yet another course of thought and actionable reality—sometimes in rapid-fire succession at the rate of twenty million bits of data per second. The continuing presentations and selections of ongoing possibilities are fed by those twenty million bits of data per second, which are then fed into our subconscious mind by our environments and our minds' filters. We spend most of our lives completely unaware of the process and the consequences of our thoughts and beliefs. Of course, there are also those milestone marker moments when our conscious thoughts are suddenly riveted upon a life-altering event or experience that is not easily forgotten and requires our additional thoughts and actions.

Considering the Law of Cause and Effect, many people believe that all life is sacred and that we should not kill and eat other mammals nor terminate other life forms because of a resultant debt. The spiritually evolved person believes that reverence for all life recognizes more than the outer shell of a body and that of an inner energy being. While some people become vegetarians for personal health reasons, some people will not support the slaughter of livestock for food but will kill mosquitoes, mice, and other life forms without regard for the consequences. And what about the fact that our daily diets also include vegetable and plant life? Many people also believe that their participation in the death of animals and their use of animal products will cause a subconscious guilty reaction that reduces the quality of their lives. In creating their reality, if they consciously or subconsciously believe something to be a problem, it will likely become manifest. So where do we draw the line with regard to what form of life, and for what purpose do we decide to kill and eat it? It is our intention that prevails rather than common sense. It's up to each of us to make the call. It's our creation and our unique virtual experience.

In looking at cause and effect, consider the meaningful, memorable events and people who come and go in our lives. Are there lessons to be learned or balances to be maintained without our knowledge or our consideration that we are unaware of? In balancing the cause and effect of our created reality, others will enter and depart from our life with exquisite timing and often with a purpose or reason beyond our knowledge or understanding. And so it is when we enter and interact with the lives of others—whether momentarily or as lifelong actors in life's drama.

An interesting aspect of our selection of actionable realities is the manner in which our selection of possibilities and our consequential actions dovetail perfectly with the varied choices and activities of countless others. In quantum physics, this is called *entanglement*. The wonders of entanglement, synchronicity, or coincidence become quite evident. The need to consider the consequences of our choices of possibilities as they affect others becomes apparent as well. When we learn to manage and direct our dominant thoughts, energies, and when we are aware of our basic beliefs, we can then choose our future from the same limitless possibilities rather than coast through life from one unhappy crisis or upset to another.

The Universal Law of Mentality posits that everything that we see and experience in our physical world originated in the mental and universal realm. This is a key to understanding how our creative universe works. All energy and matter are created and governed by a universal mind. A universal consciousness manifests all things, and our human minds are part of and linked with that universal consciousness. Both our casual thoughts and our strong, dominant thoughts are very powerful creative energies. Why not think happy, positive thoughts?

The Universal Law of Correspondence states that there is agreement and harmony that corresponds at all planes of existence—as above, so below, between spiritual, mental, and physical realms. The ancient Greek philosopher Socrates has written, "Know thyself and thou shalt know all the mysteries of the gods and the universe."

The Universal Law of Vibration tells us that everything vibrates and moves and that nothing rests. Everything in our universe is comprised of energy that vibrates at varied frequencies. The Universal Law of Attraction is based upon the axiom that energy attracts like energy. This is true throughout both the mental and physical planes of existence. Even our thoughts are a source of vibrating energy that can transform wave energy to particle—or mass energy. Oftentimes, our emotions create a faster and higher vibratory rate of energy. Examples of this are fear and love.

The Universal Law of Polarity states that everything in energy has a duality with opposite poles of polarity in the mental and physical planes of existence. There are generally two sides to everything, appearing as opposites; there is happy and unhappy, positive and negative, hot and cold, peace and war, etc. The differing extremes, however, are of the same energy but differing degrees.

The Universal Law of Rhythm states that everything in the universe vibrates and moves in certain rhythms and patterns. The rhythms establish the seasons, cycles, stages of development, and patterns of repetitions and regularity. What often appears to be random is, on the larger scale, actually very regular and orderly. Like a pendulum, that which swings in one direction will necessarily swing back in an opposite direction in time. Happy is, as happy does!

The Universal Law of Gender states that everything in creation has both a masculine and feminine principle. This is evident in human beings, plants, minerals, electrons, magnetic poles, and the like. Within each man and woman, there are latent elements of the other, and each gender has very different expressions of emotions and behaviors. It is said that when you know of this difference, you will know what it means to be a complete person.

All of the Universal Laws pertain to the causal and mental-physical realms of our existence or reality. Unconditional love however, is our experience of the human bio-electrical heart chakra system. This experience is recognized, but not produced by the human mind. Too many people believe that love is bound by the mental attributes of honor, equality, commitment, honesty, trust, respect, and sacrifice. Love however, knows no mental laws. Love takes nothing and asks for nothing in return.

We have many key assets and attributes with which to determine, create, and enhance our reality. Love and beauty are the essence of our reality.

> *Life isn't about finding yourself. Life is about creating yourself.*
>
> —GEORGE BERNARD SHAW

VI

Love and Beauty

The element of the universe that we call the unified energy field is actually an ocean of love and love is the glue that holds everything together in our universe. The love recognized within each of us is born out of a sense of oneness with all of our creation. Our human experience of love is a remarkable journey of discovery. We can enjoy all of the human emotions and excitement evoked by love, and we can also discover a new capacity within ourselves. Our capacity to love is far more important than our being loved by others. To experience being loved by others is always a joyous and wonderful thing, but it is our own sharing of unconditional love that demonstrates a lifetime example for others to follow. Love is the total identification with our beloved without indebtedness to our beloved. The deep, profound experience of love places the health, welfare, and concerns of our beloved before our very own concerns. Can you recall how people in love have been seen as deliriously happy and incredibly healthy? They were happy in both mind and heart.

The ultimate life principle for a happy and meaningful life is unconditional love and beauty. When unconditional love occupies our dominant thoughts and beliefs, our life experiences will change dramatically. Giving and sharing our gift of unconditional love provides us with the deep and lasting satisfaction of having done something absolutely wonderful with our lives. Love is either conditional or unconditional; there is nothing in between. Unconditional love is not a mental decision but is an experience over which we have no control—only an unabridged joy! To experience unconditional love for all of our creation is a partial experience of the totality of consciousness. The act of loving others unconditionally is liberating. The beloved can express his or her true being with no fear of rejection or of love being conditionally taken away. We can love the life we live. Unconditional love for others is a love for no particular reason other than the fact that we are of the same divine essence. Giving and receiving love can be both spontaneous and intentional.

When we love others, we should not hesitate to tell them so. When love is shared, it is returned, but unconditional love does not need to be returned as a reason for sharing. All too often, we mistakenly fail to separate our love for people from our disdain for their actions or behaviors. We can love them for who they are and not for what they do or don't do. With regard to others, we might recall Corinthians 13:4: "Love is patient, love is kind. It does not envy, it does not boast. It is not proud. It does not dishonor others, it is not self-seeking, love is not easily angered and it keeps no record of wrongs."

Our true identity or consciousness is that of love, and it is the perfect, most magnificent being. We need only to go within the human body to discover our true, higher selves. When we become silent listeners, all other issues and problems of the mind and body become much less important and cease to exist. This transformative discovery will also change our awareness of our lives' purposes and meanings.

Love, joy, and beauty are not only functions of our soul, but they are our inheritance and should be shared. When we become centered in love and beauty, our loving countenance will draw others to our kind, considerate, and compassionate ways. Our family members and especially our children will be the first to benefit from love. Children are the most responsive, and they learn what they live and experience. Children and young adults today experience a much more rapid growth, and they form beliefs and behaviors at a very early age. These conscious and subconscious beliefs will direct their futures. Children live what they learn, and they learn what they live and experience. Children also readily observe and sense our subtle and intentional energy displays far beyond the spoken word. When we love both children and adults, we should tell them so without reservation. It is not enough to raise our children in the same manner that we were raised because of the rapid acceleration and larger growth capacity of children. We should afford them the opportunity to realize their highest potential to levels that took us many years to realize. Imagine what this will do for future generations and the global evolution.

We can and should encourage not only children but also others to truly know themselves. We must also first discover and come to know ourselves and our beliefs. It has been said that 95 percent of the world's problems are the result of poor relationships—whether personal, familial, communal, governmental, or global. Even our national divorce rate now exceeds 52 percent, according to the National Center for Disease Control and Prevention. Of those divorced, 42 percent have remarried. Imagine what our world would be like if we all spoke from loving hearts and minds and used clear, honest communications. Recall that it is our relationships with people and things in our created reality that present an environment through which we observe, react to, and measure our personal evolutionary growth.

Not only are our words important, but the lack or absence of words can also cause heartache and regret. Have you ever wished that you had said something to another person before they had died? Often this unfinished relationship occurs when we have not cleared the slate of our misunderstandings. Why leave unsaid our feelings and loving, kind words of appreciation, forgiveness, and affection? Clear the slate now, before learning to regret not doing so. We should all leave this earthly realm as happy and contented beings.

An oriental proverb advises us to welcome everyone, including strangers, as cherished and dignified guests. All too often our relationships suffer because of our judgments and beliefs. Do you know your beliefs? Do you love yourself as equally as others? Do you truly love and appreciate all of your creation? There are so many varied questions available to determine our beliefs, and it is imperative for us to realize how our unfounded and unwanted beliefs can shape our values, our actions, and our lives. These hidden, programed beliefs further influence our dominant thoughts and prevent or delay us from raising our awareness to reach the highest levels of reality.

Consider that our true being, a perfect consciousness, is far more beautiful than anything that we could wish to become. We have an inherent wisdom of the heart. When we know our true identity, we can then also know what it is that is important for our beliefs. When we embrace the idea that love is our core essence and is central to our beliefs, we can begin to see beauty in all things. The beauty that we see or hear externally is brought to our minds and often expressed in words, but our awareness and appreciation of beauty requires no words. The beauty that we experience is simply a mirror reflection of our inner selves that are brought to our cognitive awareness. However, beauty is also a choice that we choose to make; yes, beauty is a choice in our creation. A happy open heart will choose to see beauty rather than ignore it. Remember that our attitudes and feelings impact our thoughts, and our thoughts, in turn, determine our experiences.

Beauty is believed to be obvious to us because of our capability to see and hear the pleasing harmony and patterns in nature. The language of nature is beauty, and beauty is intrinsically linked to love and joy. The soft spring breeze will whisper secrets to us if we choose to listen. Each of us can remember watching a beautiful, glowing, and red sunset or recall the song of a wren, singing its heart out to greet the dawn. Look further, we and see the love and beauty expressed when we reach out at 3 a.m. to silently touch our soul mate just to know that they are there. Will you hear the words in a song meant just for you? Hear the unexpected, new information or the timely words of another. Look closely at your emotions when you observe a loyal, loving pet or a litter of newborn kittens. The giggly laughter of a three-year-old child should be music to the ears. Rejoice in the love shared in timeless moments.

Our cognitive experience of beauty does not require any deductive or inductive analytical thought to recognize the joy found in what we have seen or heard. To be one with nature is to simply exist quietly in the present moment and become part of the flow of the universe. These are timeless moments rather than moments in time. Stop here, and recall those timeless moments that you have experienced. Did they not involve beauty, peace, joy, and love? On occasion, a tragic event or experience can also suddenly cast one into a moment of timeless shock. We can practice living in the present moments of awareness and bring about incredible changes in our lives. This is an intentional choice that we can make. Unfortunately, not everyone can or will come to the realization that love and beauty are the ultimate truths of our existence.

We can look even closer and recognize the beauty that is not always so obvious in this infinite, powerful world. The vast scope of nature is filled with turbulence, violence, death, and decay in a balanced act in the ever-changing theater of a visible and invisible universe. We can learn to appreciate a world filled with the smallest, most intricate, and most amazing life forms. Our recognition of beauty should include a true love of all forms of creation and an understanding of the interconnectedness of all things in this energy field. In the natural world, even the seemingly random acts of nature are actually in a perfect order and balance.

Whether we are looking at celestial bodies or a very small insect, the beauty and elegance of nature is far greater than the scope of manmade copies of beauty in art and science. The depictions in art that we revere as beautiful are the work of a craftsperson and only reflect the beauty that he or she sees. The piece of art then evokes the same awareness of an inner beauty in the observer. When we choose to look for and see beauty everywhere, we find it not only in those things physical but also in more subtle things—such as a silent smile, the laughter of children, the strength of the human spirit, and the marvel of synchronicity.

Love and beauty are functions of the soul. Love is never the product of the mind and cannot be taught or learned. Over many centuries, numerous poets and philosophers have tried with difficulty to describe love. They have described love using labels such as philos, eros, agape, unconditional, and transcendental. Love then begins to appear as a mental function to be decided upon and abandoned at will. Because the human mind analyzes, dissects, and categorizes everything, it is inevitable that love has been described in so many ways. Truth be told, love will more likely cause us to happily lose our rational minds. Our human minds usually destroy our loving relationships because we develop expectations of others that can't be fulfilled. Of course, over time, people change their beliefs, their values, and their behaviors, often causing an imbalance of expectations. Often, people think that they are in love and realize too late that love was never part of their mental circus. If they once had the experience of love, it was the human ego that destroyed it. This contrasts with the love that is the essence of our being. We are love. Love is our realization of the soul—much like beauty, joy, and truth. Our love is integrated with all of creation.

The Lebanese philosopher Kahlil Gibran (1883–1930) wrote this: "Love requires nothing and neither takes, nor gives anything but love. Love will not possess anything nor will love be possessed."

There is only one kind of love, and it is the shared intimacy that determines the extent of our loving relationships with everyone and everything. The love of our children is differentiated from that of our spouses by the differing levels of intimacy shared. Intimacy is not only shared with other people but also at various levels with all of our creation. Take the time to think about this for a moment. What is it that we enjoy in life at an intimate, personal level? This is our creation, our meaningful reality. We can learn to see and hold creation intimately as our own as an awakened, self-actualized person. There are neither any techniques nor any mental processes by which we can grant ourselves the acquisition or experience of love. However, love will find us when we choose to better know ourselves. When we come to know a deep and abiding love, it will be an experience beyond the description of words. It matters not to be concerned whether we are loved but to know only love for others. What others think of us is their business. Be happy in the knowledge that, to others, we are exactly who they think that we are.

How many people do we know who exist, going from one crisis to another on a daily basis? What sort of meaning have they added to their lives? They depend upon crises for value or validation of their worth. Many people become victims of their past experience and find it difficult to let go of their natural egos, and they become defensive or guarded. They often then choose a neutral position because they fear loss or emotional injury. Past emotional experiences may have challenged their trust and loving spirits. When they experienced sorrow, pain, grief, or despair, it was love that formed the basis upon which these emotions were compared. We live in a world of opposites—light and dark, positive and negative, and so forth. To the extent that we can experience love, we can also experience sorrow and pain. If we choose a neutral state that is centered between love and loss, then there is nothing gained or lost. This is an old saying by Alfred Tennyson: "Tis better to have loved and lost than never to have loved at all." When we have loved, we have never lost anything, except possibly our rational minds. The experience of love will last beyond eternal time.

It has become evident that our troubled world desperately wants and needs a major shift in consciousness and a loving, joyous message of unification, peace, and tranquility. Our present time has been described as an age of information and technology, having changed from that of manufacturing. Collectively, we are probably evolved to the level of knowledge and awareness of the third level Plato's four levels of reality. The next level in our evolutionary status is the highest level—the totality of consciousness. What are your conscious beliefs and dominant thoughts? As a global community, we are all linked by our shared concerns for humanity. Now rapidly changing and developing, our personal foundations for our lives include wisdom, kindness, understanding, compassion, and beauty. These may become our life principles. We must examine and know our beliefs and become aware of our dominant thoughts because they determine our reality. The time has come for each of us to examine our lives and strive to be examples of people living happy self-realized lives. Each of us has talents and gifts to share with others. Certainly, there must be something that we can do for others to enrich their lives.

Kabir (1440–1518), the Indian mystic poet and saint, wrote of the relevance of our human existence in his book *Ocean of Love*. Kabir noted that each of us, seen as individuals, are like single drops from the ocean. The enlightened person will know from experience that people are not single drops separated from the ocean but are one with the ocean of love and with the universe. Rumi wrote, "You are not a drop of water in an ocean, you are the entire ocean in a drop of water."

Since reality begins within our individual consciousness, each of us is then a product or creation of our own making. Examine these new ideas and understandings, and see if they don't ring true in alignment with your hopes, faith, beliefs, and knowledge. In the end, it is not about doing but about *being*. You are invited to create your intentional reality and to live and enjoy the best life possible.

> *He is the half-part of a blessed man, left to be finished*
> *such as she; and she a fair-divided excellence, whose*
> *fullness of perfection lies in him.*
>
> —WILLIAM SHAKESPEARE

VII

Beliefs and Quantum Reality

How many people truly know what their realities are or how reality has been created? Our true being is dynamic and changing. Modern philosophy is the objective study of the human psyche. The human psyche is the totality of the mind—conscious and unconscious. Our psyche is the combination of our thoughts, feelings, emotions, and motivations that direct our bodies' reactions to social and physical environments. Ancient Greek texts included the word *soul* in defining the psyche; however, our present etymology differentiates our psyche from the concept of a soul. Contemporary psychology addresses two basic levels of the human experience of reality. Conscious reality is the state of things perceived as they actually exist—including things that are, have been, and will exist. A second perceived reality is that of the unconscious and subconscious mind, which is abstract, imagined, dreamt, and delusional.

The human experience and reality has been studied for centuries, and the philosopher Plato (427–348 BC) spent years promulgating his writings on reality. Plato searched for an understanding of the nature of being. His student Aristotle referred to the study of being as metaphysics, with ontology as its central branch of study.

Whether we know it or not, our dominant thoughts and beliefs create our reality in accord with the Law of Attraction. Much of our lives are dictated by our beliefs. When we know that to be true, our trust ensures our belief and further empowers it. Plato has written that our beliefs are acquired through the five senses as experiences while knowledge is obtained through reasoning about that which is unchanging in existence. Our beliefs are about the appearance of things, while knowledge is about reality and how things really are. Plato also said that there was and is a difference between knowledge and opinion, which depends upon the human capacity for imagination, perception, and reasoning. Plato viewed reality as having four graduated levels of human experience. The lowest level of reality was described as that of illusion. Whether dreaming while asleep or enjoying imaginative mental flights of fantasy, illusion was thought to be a valid human experience of any duration. This level of reality was believed to be the prominent reality of mentally disturbed persons and many elderly people residing within a physical body. Some of today's pharmaceutical drugs can also induce a state of illusionary reality.

The second level of reality was described by Plato as an informed awareness of observations and perceptions received by way of our five physical senses. Some people today spend much of their lives believing that their realities are totally dependent upon their five bodily senses, which provide them with a focused awareness. Their realities are experiences that consist primarily of that which is seen, heard, smelled, tasted, and touched with the physical body. The human experience of the senses can alternately be mixed with that of illusion. Hedonistic pleasures are those of maximized sensual experiences.

Higher yet, the third level of reality was that of eudaimonism—the experience of a personal knowledge and belief system acquired through critical thinking. The human experience or reality, with an expanded knowledge and practices, would include inductive and deductive reasoning with abstract ideas and concepts. This level of reality and human experience will necessarily prompt a personal search for purpose as well as the origins of the human consciousness and self-actualization. An increased personal knowledge will most certainly advance our beliefs and our reality as multisensory beings.

The highest level of reality is the ultimate experience of awareness beyond the functions of logic, reasoning, and knowledge. This level is beyond illusion, imagination, perception, and sensory information; this is a reality of a divine experience of God. This level of experience is where and when we meet and acknowledge our higher selves as if looking in a mirror. Our experiences of our higher selves occur when the physical body and the soul are aligned and communicating. Today, this phenomenon is commonly called *the totality of consciousness*. It is my belief that quantum reality will include all of these progressive levels of the human experience. The energy of our dominant thoughts and our beliefs is the creative force of reality.

Because our purpose in life is to create our unique, individual realities and to then happily enjoy our experiences, we can readily employ our unique, human talents and our capabilities to do so. Made in the image of the universal Creator, we are conscious beings inhabiting a temporary human body and mind to create and enjoy our experiences. It is as simple as that! The four levels of created and experienced realities satisfy the religious and the scientific definition of creation. Our life experience should be based upon how we've loved and touched the hearts of others.

> *How contentedly I view any room containing you. In fact I care not where you be, just as long as it's with me.*
>
> —Ogden Nash

VIII

The Mind and Consciousness

The most important functional element of our experiential levels of reality is that of our human awareness. It is human awareness that moves humans through the process of a vertical path of evolutionary growth in consciousness. Bear with me for a moment. You are aware now that you are reading this book. You are also aware of your location and position while reading. More importantly, you are also aware of your awareness. Are you now or have you been acutely aware of those times when you experienced fantasies, illusions, and exaggerated imaginings? Are you also aware of your sensual reality? Lastly, are you now, or have you been aware of the level of realities that you created for yourself?

Look to Plato's higher level of a personal knowledge with inductive and deductive reasoning and critical thinking. Are you aware now of this level of your personal experience? When we experience the totality of consciousness, we will reach the pinnacle of human awareness. Hopefully, our lives will all progress upward and achieve expanded levels of awareness and consciousness. Our role here on earth includes our inherent and acute human awareness as necessary to ascend to our true eternal reality.

Throughout history, science and religion have been diametrically opposed and at odds with each other regarding the basic purpose of life and life's processes. More recently, the sciences have not only documented but have also substantiated and supported the doctrines and principles of religion. The sciences can now determine and explain in detail the esoteric phenomena that operate in both our physical and nonvisible universe. Moreover, science is without a moral agenda and is probably much better at describing and documenting the workings of our wondrous universe than the secretive religious societies. Our present human state of evolution and spirituality requires that we have adequate dialogue and answers for a continued evolutionary growth.

Tomorrow changes the face of reality. Reality is our experiences—the living, responsive flow of experiences that continues eternally on many levels or planes of existence. We now know that our human awareness and consciousness is causal and defines our existence and our reality. Our minds, with volition, and our consciousness are as much a fundamental component of the quantum nature of the universe as are the elementary particles and forces. In 1899, Max Planck (1858–1947) first introduced the quantum theory; however, the very idea and concept of atoms was controversial and certainly not acceptable to the general public at that time. The message regarding that which we think we are still has huge implications for each of us in our ongoing searches for personal identity and growth. Beyond the standard model of physics, quantum theory proves to be both challenging and rewarding in the search for an understanding of the workings of the universe in our everyday lives. We create our illusionary, physical reality with our minds! Max Planck, Nobel Prize recipient and theoretical physicist, said, "All matter originates and exists only by virtue of a force which brings the particle of an atom to vibration and holds this most minute solar system of the atom together. We must assume behind this force the existence of a conscious and intelligent mind. This mind is the matrix of all matter." The human mind with creative thought provides the resonant energy to construct and govern all physical matter and light.

Each of us has the potential for a happy, richly rewarding life experience of our own making. We were meant to be free, to be courageous in exploring and uncovering the vastness of our being and the sometimes hidden aspects of a full life experience. We will not be complete without experiencing happiness, sadness, joy, mystery, fear, thrills, sorrow, compassion, love, joy, and peace. It is our human mind that is cognizant of these emotional experiences which originated from our hearts.

Many people are unaware of the immense power of the human mind and consciousness. The basic scientific elements of the human consciousness are attention, awareness, perception, cognition, imagination, and memory. Attention is best described as the probe of awareness. Our awareness will focus on where we put our attention. For example, your attention at this moment is directed at these words before you, yet you are simultaneously aware of the voices in your head and the fact that you are reading. We can direct our attention wherever we wish—whether it is an internal or external experience. Through concentrated meditation or introspection, we can reverse the direction of our attention of the physical world, toward the silent realm of consciousness. Our attention can be withdrawn from the outward experience to the inward to the one doing the experiencing. This capability belongs only to us as human beings. External sights, sounds, scents, and other things can also attract and hold our attention without our intention to have them do so. I have previously mentioned the fact that our attention feeds approximately forty bits of information per second into our cognitive awareness, but we will likely remember only a very small portion of this information. On another level, our attention feeds more than twenty million bits of information per second to be programmed into our subconscious mind, according to Bruce Lipton in his 2005 book, *The Biology of Belief*. There is no way that the wakeful, conscious human mind can accommodate twenty million bits of information per second.

Our beliefs result in our behavioral habits. We act consciously and subconsciously. When the conscious mind is busy with thoughts of the past and the future, the subconscious mind runs our lives as if on autopilot. It even drives the car when we become distracted or inattentive. The incredible amount of information to our brains is necessary in providing the data required for the multitude of possibilities in choosing our realities. But what if our original beliefs were incorrect or no longer relevant? Our actions would likely not be appropriate.

The incredible amount of information coming into our brains is necessary in providing the data required for choosing our actionable realities. Through concentrated meditation and introspection, we can reverse the direction of our attention from the physical world to the silent, inner realm of consciousness. Our attention can be withdrawn from the external experience and turned to the inward experience and the experiencer. This capability of meditation and introspection belongs only to us as human beings.

Plato's third level of reality and informed awareness includes the factors of hope, faith, and knowledge. Hope is defined as a feeling—the expectation and desire for a certain thing to happen. With hope, we trust that something might occur without, or beyond our control. Hope is much like desiring or wishing. Without faith or knowledge, some people must depend only upon hope. For others, hope is not an option or a plan. Hope may often lead to disappointment and a loss of faith. Hope is a lack of certainty or knowing. Whether hope is stronger than fear depends upon the individual and his or her beliefs. Having experienced mortal fear on numerous occasions, many of us would never resort to, or depend upon hope to be part of our survival. No amount of hope will provide the adequate knowledge or desired circumstances.

Faith can be defined as believing in something, even if it is something unknown or uncertain. Faith is the foundation of most of the world's religions. Faith is often based upon spiritual apprehension rather than absolute proof or experiential knowledge. Faith is a complete trust or confidence in something or someone. Faith is like the cement that indemnifies a belief and insulates the belief from closer introspection. Faith is also an intentional and mental state of mind rather than a creative action. For centuries, faith, hope, and charity have been necessary elements of organized religion. These concepts helped control the masses and distract them from a personal, knowledgeable awareness. It is our experiential knowledge and experience that will shape our identity and determine our ultimate reality. Why not an open, loving, happy experience?

Our human awareness is essential and is the most important element of our consciousness in forming, discovering, and changing our beliefs. Our conscious and subconscious beliefs are not always based on facts but on our perception of events and experiences of which we were aware. There is a level of collective consciousness for various populations of the world. Human consciousness makes humans sentient beings with the innate ability to perceive and to feel a subjective experience. Sentience distinguishes between thinking, or reasoning, and feeling, or sensing. As sentient beings, we have the capacity to be aware of something thought to be deep within each of us, and we are aware of our awareness. It is believed by the scientific community that no other mammal or creature has this unique capability to be aware of an innate awareness or to think things through with an attendant level of emotion. Scientific research has also shown that bottlenose dolphins, great apes, orcas, elephants, and magpies have all demonstrated that they possess self-awareness and a limited comprehension. However, they have not demonstrated a higher intellect or a deeper awareness of their awareness.

Perception allows us to recognize only a small portion of the information that we receive in our wakeful consciousness. Consider our very limited human eyesight as an element of our perception. Our eyes are sensitive to a very narrow band of light in the enormous range of light frequencies. In our physical realm, we can see less than 1 percent of the electromagnetic spectrum, and we hear less than 1 percent of the acoustic spectrum. Even colors that we believe we observe are only our physiological and psychological responses to wavelengths of light entering our eyes. Supposedly, it is our eyes that filter light frequencies and assigned them with perceived colors. We lack the visual acuity of an eagle, and we do not have the capability of night vision used by other mammals. These attributes are not necessary in creating our experiences.

Another scientific premise holds that everything that we think that we see is actually projected from our creative minds outward through our eyes. Human life is a colorful, textured movie of which humans are the directors. Consider this: we believe that we see a movie or video externally at ten to twelve frames per second, but we actually project our created, perceived views with the same frame frequency. Our timed viewing and our projection are however, seamless. In our physical realm, we tend to believe that some tactile information is generated externally from our bodily senses of sight, hearing, taste, smell, and touch. Until we know the difference, our minds automatically filter this sensory information subjectively comparing any new data with that of our past experiential knowledge and our beliefs. This is the external illusion. Know that we do not smell, taste, feel, or hear anything until our brain informs us of the sensation. The entire tactile experience occurs within our heads and our minds as we experience our creation. If someone were to suggest the existence of the smell of fresh, buttered popcorn, we could actually smell it, even if it was not present. Even the suggestion of a tasty food can cause us to begin to salivate.

Consider too that we will have a dream experience with our eyes closed where the sensory information of the five bodily organs emanates. In our dreams, the sights, sounds, touches, and emotions are a very real experience in our lowest level of consciousness. It appears that we humans have a great neural network with our sensory vision being the weaker element.

Furthermore, our multisensory perception includes experiences other than those brought to us through our five senses. Our mental perception of ideas, plans, dreams, and concepts are critical to our existence. To a very large degree, our perception is dependent upon our capacity for imagination. Human perception influences and controls both behavior and gene activity. Our brains and nervous systems interpret environmental stimuli and send signals to our cells. Our cells then respond to support our activity in our perceived environment. Our human perception is also very important in seeing and recognizing the realities that each of us creates. Far too many people see their external realities but do not fully realize that they have created these realities with their dominant beliefs and thoughts.

Become the authority in your life. We own our destiny. Our beliefs are the hidden force that creates our virtual reality. It was Henry Ford who once said this: "If you believe you can or believe you can't, you're right." It was evident that if I could think something, then I could do it. Can you remember a narrow-minded person that you have known that refused to see or accept anything new or challenging? People with limited beliefs will not likely see the advantage of the infinite possibilities available for their lives. Theirs is the case of a life-altering limited perception. Usually, these people refuse to accept new ideas because of their hidden, unknown subconscious beliefs or their lack of imagination. We can only make suggestions to them and allow them the dignity of their troubles and chosen path. When we condition our minds with our beliefs to see and accept new information, we will be open and amenable to critical thinking and learning. It has been said that curiosity is a sign of intelligence. It is quite natural for the human mind to become curious and analytical, using both inductive and deductive reasoning. This is how we examine and question the validity of information we receive. This function of the mind is also that which Plato described as the third level of reality—that of informed reasoning and critical thinking.

There is an interesting relationship that develops between our capacity for perception and the development of our beliefs and values. Our beliefs are the most powerful component of our natures, and they provide a moral framework with guiding principles, preferences, and prejudices that impact our perception and our behaviors. Once formed, unfounded and false beliefs may be difficult to change and will limit our potential. Biased beliefs will cause us to see and experience only that which we wish to see.

Our socialization is a lifelong process of inheriting, forming, and changing our norms, customs, ideologies, and beliefs. Our beliefs are formed from infancy and vary depending upon exposure to immediate family, friends, teachers, community norms, geographical locations, education, and our social and work environments. Many of our conscious and subconscious beliefs are false and unfounded because they have been formed from emotion—primarily that of fear. Although they may not be false, some beliefs may be of little or no value. Our values are based upon what is important and acceptable to us. Our values and our mental attitudes, with attendant emotions, will likely dictate some of our beliefs and behaviors. Hopefully, we will understand why it is important to learn about our subconscious beliefs as well as our conscious beliefs. With a positive and powerful belief system, there is no limit to what humans can achieve in this world.

I have suggested that our beliefs and our virtual experiences have been influenced systematically by the words of our parents, teachers, friends, and others. As humans, our beliefs and behaviors are programmed by habituation and memory. As infants, we came into life pure, innocent, and vulnerable. We were subject to being entertained by adults with their ideas and values—adults who often waved baby rattles and toys in our faces. Our actions as infants were guided only by our instincts and emotions. Within the first year of our lives, we gradually became aware of ourselves and began to gather limited knowledge and develop a belief system. We also began to develop our human egos. In these formative years, we begin to develop a collection of information and to adopt the values of countless others. We are never told of the virtual reality created by the structures of community beliefs and norms.

Both our perceptions and our beliefs are flexible and changing. Our beliefs then become a filter for our perceptions of information and our experiences. As we grow older and more experienced, the reverse can occur, and our perceptions can influence our beliefs. With awareness, we can determine and control our beliefs, thoughts, actions, and futures. We can create our tomorrows—our destinies! We are much more than a collection of social and moral values, beliefs, and choices.

Human perception is the key to our reality at two levels. Not only can our perceptions influence our beliefs, but our bodies' cells also have receptor proteins that send environmental signals to our bodies' cells. Human thoughts traveling throughout our bodies are the strongest environmental signal. Do you remember Dr. Marsh's findings that describe the human brain creating a three-dimensional world? Our thoughts and our beliefs will impact nearly all the functions of our bodies. Our bodies' cells are listening to and reacting and interacting with our thoughts and beliefs. Be aware of what you think because your body is listening. It has been medically documented that we can make ourselves sick and unhealthy with our unfounded fears and beliefs. Our beliefs and our thoughts can cause the placebo effect or the reverse nocebo effect to occur in our bodies. The nocebo effect is described by the Oxford Dictionary as a harmless substance or a negative thought that creates a harmful effect in the person taking or experiencing it. Perhaps our human awareness should first include an awareness of what humans are—silent, aware, electromagnetic energy beings.

Our human awareness is central to our growing consciousness and is the most important element in connecting us to a creative, universal intelligence. Awareness is the key to the correlative relationship between our consciousness and our physical reality. It's worth repeating that consciousness is awareness without thought. Moreover, our human awareness does not depend upon and is not created by the human brain. Actually, there are two aspects of our human awareness. It is our cognitive awareness in a wakeful state that allows us to be cognizant and mindful of our immediate thoughts and the sensations received through our five physical senses. This is how we construct and experience the "I" of our being. But even our mindful thoughts and our physical attributes are very much like the wearing of a jacket on the physical body. The real self—the silent, energy body—is simply wearing the physical and mental jacket for this realm of reality.

All creatures have varied levels of awareness, but only humans have evolved to the extent that we are aware of our awareness. For example, an insect has a basic awareness that allows it to recognize fire as a threat. Depending upon their level of evolution, many other life forms are aware of threats to their survival. Much like humans, some animals have the basic emotions of fear and affection, but only humans as sentient beings appear to possess a capacity for a deep and profound love.

Any parts of our reality that occur in the physical and mental realms are a production of our human mind powered by consciousness. Above the physical and mental realms of consciousness are the finer realms described by Plato and other philosophers and poets.

When we begin to examine and become aware of our beliefs, thoughts, and actions, we awaken in a profound way. We can awaken our bodies' cells to a new order of life and possibilities. The "who" that we think we are will change.

For those of us who have come to know that there is another realm of existence beyond death, we also know that our awareness and consciousness do not die but continue on to other dimensions or realms beyond the physical plane of existence. The after-death experience will depend upon our level of awareness and our beliefs.

Consider that I have dedicated this book to my wife, not necessarily her memory. It is my belief that she yet watches over me from another realm. She will also communicate with me and has advised me to try to become a more kind and gentle man. Our physical world is but a small part of the surrounding astral realm. We create our own virtual reality not only in our physical experience but also when we leave the physical body for another realm. What happens is exactly that which we wish to happen. If not by our intent or design, then our experiences after death will be created by our uncontrolled and subconscious thoughts. There is also an experience after death that is created by a collective consciousness if our personal awareness and intent is insufficient.

I believe that death is an illusion for the earth-bound. The death of our physical bodies is not to be feared; death has no dominion over us. Upon the death of our human bodies, we simply transfer energy bodies to move to a higher realm. If we believe in a realm or a place called hell, then it will be exactly as we have thought it to be. If we create another reality formed by more favorable beliefs, then it will also be much as we believed it to be. Be advised that there is no place "out there" called heaven or hell. Heaven and hell are not destinations but are states of awareness—or simply mental relationships with the realm of wave and particle matter energies. In short, heaven is exactly what we wish to think of it and make of it. How many people do we know who have made their lives a living hell on this earth? Heaven is also available on demand. Create it now before you need it.

On a related note, recall this expression: "My life flashed before my eyes." When we leave our bodies immediately after physically dying, we cross over into another realm of awareness where there is no time as we now know it. The visual flash of our entire life is not a linear series of time-line images but a total, instant, and simultaneous awareness of all life events. This vision—or sudden revelation—is the same timeless experience of the "now" of time from which we have created our reality. That sudden flash of awareness also includes a complete, comprehensive understanding of seeing the events and their consequences. At the time of our physical deaths, the panoramic views of our lives will not be used for judgment, contrary to popular belief and church teachings. The instant overview will serve to show us no right or wrong but will instead show us how we could have acted differently to cause less harm, injury, and insult to others. After having experienced some of these things, how can anyone then be apprehensive or fearful of physical death? While still alive physically, our fears are primarily those of a sense of impending loss or fear of the unknown.

After our physical bodies die, we immediately see, know, and understand the consequences of our previous actions as those actions related to others—particularly any harm we have caused. The universe requires a balance in all matters. Our energy bodies then continue on to other realms. Although devoid of tissue matter, our consciousness or energy bodies retain intelligence and memory. Those who fear physical death most likely fear what they perceive as a loss of attachments in the earthly realm. Their valued attachments are more than those things physical—such as their feelings, emotions, habits, mental comforts, and companionship—and they can't take the attachments with them when they depart from the earth.

The human capacity for imagination is obviously another important element in creating our beliefs and our futures. Human imagination is a form of concentrated attention, and our imagination is often the initiator of intent. Intent or willpower is unique only to the human species of mammals. Because our intent is a powerful creative force, at no other time do we exercise our willpower. Even in our subconscious dreams, we have no discretionary intent but only respond to circumstances coming sequentially in our dreams. Have you ever considered the root word of *image* in using your imagination? And what are the images made of? Many people believe that human imagination creates only images and unreal fantasies. Some people will report that they have very little or no imagination. It may be that these persons did not develop adequate alpha brain waves to nourish the capacity for creating imagination. Unfortunately, many others simply believe that they don't have time for or any use for imaginative nonsense. As a powerful creative resource, our imagination produces images, new ideas, and energy creations. Why not happy, positive, loving ideas and beliefs?

In actuality, our imaginings are energy forms and are creating the future of us doing the imagining. Our use of imagination allows each of us to be both the creator and the experiencer of our virtual reality. Our human capacity of imagination allows us to not only visualize the future but also allows for the creation of that same future. For example, our imagination can allow us to seek and examine a variety of possible life purposes rather than simply imagining a single purpose. Quantum mechanics requires a measure of imagination to be able to begin to understand that there is nothing solid and permanent in the physical universe. There are only infinite possibilities waiting for actualization by our imagination and our intent. As we believe, so we shall think. As we think, so shall we speak and act. Imagination is the passport to change both our futures and our created selves. The people remembered throughout history as being successful have had vision; they have used their imaginations for great accomplishments. The very least we can do for ourselves is to imagine a happy and meaningful life. Where our attention goes, energy flows. A meaningful life experience with a happy heart should include positive, loving beliefs and values. The probability of illness, disease, and death is not a part of our genetic determinism. We create our reality with our beliefs, our dominant thoughts, and our creative imaginings. Too many people readily say this: "Oh, I can't imagine that."

Consider another view of the consequence of our beliefs and dominant thoughts. In each and every nanosecond of our lives, we select or design our immediate futures from a multitude of possibilities. With each ever-changing possibility, we unconsciously select and determine yet another course of thought and actionable reality, sometimes in rapid-fire succession. The continuing presentations and selections of ongoing possibilities are fed by those twenty million bits of data per second that are fed into our subconscious mind by our environment. We sometimes spend most of our lives being completely unaware of the process and the consequences of our thoughts and beliefs. Of course, there are those milestone moments when our conscious thoughts are suddenly riveted upon a life-changing event or experience that is not easily forgotten and requires our additional thoughts and actions.

An interesting aspect of our selection of our actionable realities is the manner in which our selection of possibilities and our consequential actions dovetail perfectly with the varied choices and activities of countless others. In quantum physics, this is called *entanglement*. The wonders of entanglement, synchronicity, or coincidence become quite evident. Also apparent is our need to consider the consequences of our choices of possibilities as our choices and actions affect others. When we learn to manage and direct our dominant thought energies, and when we are aware of our basic beliefs, we can then choose our futures from the same limitless possibilities rather than coast through life from one crisis to another.

Scientific research has shown that our brains are an electrical force field within the larger universal magnetic-electric force field. Much like our thoughts, our beliefs are also measurable electrical-informational properties. Once we are aware that our beliefs and our dominant thoughts determine our future, we can take the responsibility to attract even more positive changes in our lives. It is also worth noting that our imagination is closely related to our capacity for perception. Observe closely that most people who are imaginative are also very open-minded and curious and have an enlarged perception of most everything. These folks have the ability to see unlimited possibilities—they are free! Remember too, that the energy field around our mind also interacts synergistically with the energy field about our hearts.

There is another freedom experienced by many people, particularly those deeply involved with Christianity. Some experience a supernatural peace as a peace beyond the human mind and heart. Some have a spiritual freedom from earthly cares, worries, and rational logic and reasoning.

In the earliest pre-Christian era, the Chinese sought spiritual freedom in oneness with the Tao—a nameless, faceless, formless power of the universe. Taoism continues yet today.

In the Christian Bible, Philippians 4:7 describes a peace of God that surpasses all understanding. This peace and freedom has been described as so wondrous that it surpasses all human understanding. Some of us have witnessed family members and friends, in their final moments of life, suddenly experience a supernatural, peaceful surrender and freedom from all cares and concerns. Know too that the same profound, supernatural peace is available to us now in our wakeful consciousness.

The whole of our human consciousness includes the element of the superconscious. The superconscious, also known as the higher consciousness, is the raised consciousness of a human being who has reached a higher level of evolutionary development of human awareness and reality. Super consciousness occurs by human evolution and is developed with spiritual knowledge and a mental proficiency brought about by spiritual practices. When a human being evolves to the level of awareness wherein he or she is living in harmony within the unified energy field, that person is then *connected* with the source of all things. This has been called God consciousness, Christ consciousness, Buddha consciousness, cosmic consciousness, and the totality of consciousness. Having ascended to this higher level of consciousness, a human being becomes totally aware of all of creation. Enlightenment at this level is also described as being one with God. The truly enlightened person is believed to have transcended the causal level of karmic activity and the realm of morality held by the common populace.

There are some initiates and highly aware people who describe the whole of consciousness as resembling an ascending matrix. It is the human mind that is the matrix and entrance to this level of super consciousness and that is available to anyone, but very few people seek or reach this level of totality of consciousness. But this too is changing. Looking back at Plato's four levels of reality, we can see now that we all create our unique realities in the three lowest levels and attempt to reach the fourth level of the totality of consciousness. As we develop and revise our beliefs, we increase and intensify the creative force of reality.

Psychology partially defines consciousness as our capacity for thought, cognition, volition, or will power, emotion, and sensation. The combination of these elements allows us to change and expand our conscious awareness. At any given moment in our lives, our consciousness is in a *state of being*. Even while sleeping, we create and enter an altered state of being and can experience various emotions and other sensations in events that appear to be so very real. All of our experiences in the physical body and our experiences of the mind are experienced as temporary states of being in conscious awareness. When we identify ourselves with our egos, we expose ourselves to the random, changing influences of others and to the events occurring about us. We are then experiencing a state of mind as opposed to a centered, calm state of being.

There are several levels of human consciousness, and we all function at one or more of these levels simultaneously. The various levels of consciousness are not stratified with exact boundaries separating each level but instead overlap to varying degrees. The first level of consciousness is that of the gross physical plane of our existence. This is the level of our sensory awareness. The next and second level is the astral plane. The astral plane also contains the akashic field—a cosmic field containing the memory and information of all things that ever existed. Even thought energy has been retained here. Ever higher, the next level—or causal plane—is often referred to as *the universal mind.* These first three lower realms of human consciousness are restricted to the human mind and the man-made linear experience of time and space. It is meditation that allows the human being to access higher levels of awareness, consciousness, and dimensions beyond description, space, and time. Do you think about time?

This universe is not outside of you. Look inside yourself, everything that you want, you already are.

—Rumi

IX

It's About Time

This thing we call time is a fabulous commodity. In creating our virtual reality, we first create time then attempt to manage that time. We usually announce that there is never enough time. The time that we spend with our loved ones and with our personal pursuits provides a measureable experience. We won't necessarily see the experience as measureable, but what we observe as the element of time is measureable. Of course, we can also experience timeless moments. How can this be? Can we actually stop time? Time perception is a field of study within psychology and neuroscience that refers to the subjective experience of time. There is a medical term called *tachypsychia*. This is a neurological condition that alters our perception of time, often called the *tachypsych*, because of the slow-motion effect experienced when caused by extreme stress or drug abuse. Our concept of time is nothing more than a mental construct in a virtual reality, yet it is very difficult to get our minds around the concept until we actually experience the timeless now.

Time, as we know and use it, is measured by our perception of the duration of indefinite and continuously unfolding events. Time is our measurement of change and the duration of perceived movement. Our measurement tools are contrived to record and describe our experience of change or movements. The concept of time defines our reality because time allows for the sequential changes that we experience in our wakeful consciousness. Time is also referred to as duration. Duration is measured by motion or a change of position. Prior to the advent of clocks, early astronomers used duration, or motion, to determine and chart the movement of heavenly bodies in the sky. Motion, or movement, was then measured by shadows on a sundial, the movement of the moon and stars, pendulum swings, and the seasons that rhythmically come and go. Of course, quantum mechanics has determined that both time and motion are illusions as the quantum universe is static, or stationary, until movement and change is created by our beliefs and thoughts. Time is a phenomenon projected from within our heads to accommodate our reality in ten to twelve frames per second. We even think in time; the human mind requires time to think and to sequence our linked thoughts and occurrences.

When viewing external activity and movies, our eyes and brain combination can accommodate one hundred frames per second, but the images will be distorted and will appear jerky. Our perception of time may be slowed or hastened—such as when we are skydiving or facing life-threatening situations. Our experience of a sense of awe can lengthen or slow time and other human emotions can either slow or hasten time. The past, the now, and the future exist simultaneously, so I have developed a habit of viewing my time as a linear line or ribbon running just past, but close to my left side. From my position in the now of time, I manage my time by placing my appointments and other activities on the ribbon while I leave other seemingly unimportant activities to occur randomly on the ribbon. To the extent that my memory allows, I can also look backward at will to review and remember past events on the ribbon. Admittedly, my time ribbon has grown much shorter with my advancing age even though I fully understand that time is a concept.

Interestingly, the experience of time slows when measured further away from our planet earth's gravitational field. Astronauts that spent many months in space did not age as quickly as residents on the earth and the astronauts have observed time to pass more slowly in outer space and not because they were bored. Astronauts venturing to outer space and a differing time realm must make the appropriate adjustments in contrast to earth time. Here on earth, the more activity that we schedule into a measure of time, the faster time appears to occur. Scientists have researched aspects of the space-time continuum and can predict that from a set of twins, one individual having traveled two years into deep space will have aged only two years, while the twin remaining here on earth will have aged fifty years. That which we call time is distorted on the space-time continuum of our surrounding cosmos. Also, time is space, and space is time—each inversely proportionate to the other. More of one is less of the other. Those astronauts mentioned earlier traded a large measure of movement and space for a smaller measure of time.

Notice also that our sense or perception of consciousness is timeless awareness without thought; we can stop time. Being in the timeless now is called being in the specious present. Meditation, for example, can alter our perception of elapsed time. For some, a few minutes in meditation may seem like hours, but for others, an hour may seem to be only minutes. Meditation can allow us to slow our experience of time until we reach the timeless now. Drugs and alcohol will also alter or distort our sense of time. Sadly enough, even the extremes of old age in humans will slow their experience of time. Nearly all seniors will also experience both the loss of memory of time past, and will easily lose track of time present, not knowing the date and day of the week. They may also lose any recognition of a future time. Without a recollection of time past as well as no future plans, they live in the specious present, or the now of time.

Early Greek philosophers and poets believed that because of time, the human experience of happiness was totally dependent upon memory. However, we have come to know that happiness and other experiences may occur in the now of time to be remembered long after and in another time. Imagine being instantly surprised and happy with a sudden gift of a bouquet of flowers. Or imagine your experience of the instant impact of dreadful news. Our experiences are not dependent upon memory but are usually held there for some time after.

There is an old tale of two very religious and proper monks walking across the countryside. They then came upon a swollen steam. Beside the steam was a beautiful young woman who was crying. When asked why she was crying, she said that she wished to cross the stream but did not wish to ruin her only pair of shoes and her garment. The older monk smiled broadly with great happiness and suddenly swept her up, carried her across the water, and placed her on dry ground. Later, as the two monks continued walking along, the younger monk stopped and asked, "How is it that you, a celibate and pious monk, thoroughly enjoyed carrying that beautiful young woman?" The old monk replied, "I only carried her but for a brief happy moment, but it is you that continues to carry her for hours."

The concept and structure of time is built into our thoughts, language, and our behaviors. Time is a mental construct and does not exist in quantum physics. It can be said that time is only the measurement of the change in matter and our thoughts as the observer. It is not time that is altered or changed, but it is the state of matter that is changed. The equations and theories of physics cannot tell us which events are occurring right now; these events are like a map without the you-are-here arrow. The theoretical map of time does not have a now, nor does it have a flow or direction of time. All moments and events are equally real. The past, the present, and the future are simultaneously available for our mental sequencing of change, and this includes our past lives. Try putting that on your time ribbon. In the theory of relativity, the past, the present, and the future exist together simultaneously in a four-dimensional continuum of space and time. Even our thoughts require time. Because virtual reality time is typically viewed as a continual, forward, and linear progression, it is usually believed that time moves forward because the universe is still expanding outward, or changing, which is called *entropy*. In short, our very human existence requires constantly changing time and space in a physical universe. Like all mental concepts and structures, time is useful though fleeting and will eventually collapse.

There is no time element, and there is no beginning or end to our virtual reality. The "all" of everything just is. Without time, the past and the future exist only in the now as quantum possibilities for our experience. We can experience tomorrow only because we have created time. Even that which we think of as forever is right now. Just prior to her passing, my wife experienced a visionary reality and reported that I would soon join her in the afterlife. The "soon" that she referred to, is simply my continued construct of linear time. The entropy or changes occurring in my time will eventually cease in my mind as well as my projected virtual experience. She, of course, exists in the ever-present timeless now.

Consider also, the times when you have experienced déjà vu. This French expression means "already seen." Because we create our experiences in our minds, it is not difficult to imagine that we can inadvertently experience the sensation of having a repeated experience that was previously created in the same manner as time passed. Déjà vu is likely just a glitch in our time mechanism that doesn't match our memory. We create the illusion of time in order to sequence all of our events and experiences. In quantum physics, linear time as we use it does not exist. The space-time continuum does not happen; however, space-time exists, created for our delayed mental constructs.

Recall this expression: "Time slips away." Because time does not exist, the reality is that the only thing slipping away is our memory of the sequential experience. It sometimes appears that as time moves in one direction, our memory goes in the opposite direction. A very simple example of the relationship between time and change is that of a pile of sand on the desert floor. Time will then allow for change to impact the pile of sand through the wind, rain, and other disturbances. The change—or entropy—cannot be reversed. It has been said of time that we can use an egg to make an omelet, but we cannot then use an omelet to make an egg. Our constructed time is irreversible. Some people incorrectly believe that we can revisit times past and change history. If, for example, we have in the past experienced having hurt another's feelings, we cannot turn back time and redo that experience. We can revisit the experience in our memory and create another imagined experience, but the original experience cannot be changed because of a paradox wherein all inter-related aspects would also require a revision not possible. Our perceived past is unchangeable. There are, however, some poor souls who mentally continue to live in the past, all the while existing and trying to function in the present now. The people who recall the past as "a better time" are often thought to be living in the past but are actually doing so in the now of time. Their past, future, and now are simultaneously available.

In the now of time, there are no problems. There are only answers. This is where we will find truth, joy, and the true nature of our selves. Step out of the time-space continuum as this is not where you will discover all available realities. With the same mind that created our imaginary concept of time, we must consider what we do to our physical and spatial experience. After all, time and space are on the same continuum. Imagine the little neighbor boy who would greet you with his extended middle finger salute each morning as you leave the house. What takes him but two seconds of time to complete can cause you hours of thought. Have you ever sat through a concert and felt that it lasted for four agonizing hours? The reverse is also true of our construct of time. Recall the enjoyment of conversing with a dear friend or lover for hours only to find that it felt very brief and short and passed all too quickly. The length of one minute will have a different meaning depending upon which side of the bathroom door you're on. Notice too that things experienced in time will never remain the same because of change. This is because of our relative position in the *now of time*. Can you recall having awakened from sleep without any knowledge of the present time or of how long you might have slept? Usually, within a few seconds, we once again reposition ourselves on the clock of time in our virtual reality to continue our affairs. Oftentimes, I have awakened from a brief nap only to believe that I had slept into the next day still fully dressed.

As you read these words, even your thoughts immediately fade into the past and into history. Between what we call the past and the future is the now of time. Imagine that you are positioned on the razor-sharp edge of the now line. Even our thoughts about the future require a measure of time. When we learn to abandon our mental thought process, we can exist in the now of time and in awareness without thought. It is from this position in the now that we have created our history as well as our future. Everything in our lives has been and is now created from a timeless moment in the now. It is often difficult to realize that even our description of the future or the prospect of forever, exist now and have no bearing in time. Because our conception and our utilization of time have been with us for so many years since our births, it is now very difficult to grasp and fully realize the true nature of our imagined concept of time in which we sequence our creation and events. Once we have experienced a timeless now, it becomes easier to grasp and understand the true nature of time.

Anything experienced in the past from our position in the now is unchangeable history, and those things not yet experienced in the future of our time are only possibilities not yet seen or experienced. From the position of now, we can even look back in our creation of time and recall previous experiences once again. The further that we look back in time with our memory, the less we will remember. Also from our location in the now of time, we can look forward to future experiences by connecting to the conscious universe and its unlimited possibilities. This is the knowledge that allows us to create our future experiences with our minds and our intentions. The concept of time and structured events in time are a product of our minds!

Everything that has ever been or will be is available now because we exist only in the now of time. The precise moment of existence in the now is less than a nanosecond in time, and the now of our time is constantly changing with the twenty million bits of information per second that come into our subconsciousness to perpetuate change. Our minds and our consciousness are fundamental elements of the quantum reality and the universe.

There is another phenomenon experienced by many of us in our older years. Think of time as a teeter-totter, with the center fulcrum as the now of our time. There is usually a large imbalance, with our perspective of the past being much larger than our perspective of the future. As we get older and develop memory problems, the imbalance begins to grow smaller very quickly. At some point in time, or sooner or later (pun intended), we could have absolutely no past, no memories, no vision, and no plan for the future. Quite possibly, we will eventually run out of both the future as well as the past and come to experience the constant now of time—or living in the moment. The now of our concept of time is where it all begins and ends, as consciousness does not require human thoughts. Eternity too, begins and ends now.

Is there really chaos in quantum theory, as described by physicists? *Entropy* is the term for the range of chaos and disorder in a system. Chaos also includes change with the unexpected and the unpredictable. Quantum theory provides a mathematical description of the dual particle and wave behaviors and the interactions of energy and matter. Quantum mechanics demonstrate that the best that can be determined are the probabilities of matter's existence. Because quantum theory is based upon statistical probabilities, we cannot have a deterministic universe in which we can know the changing position and momentum of every atom at any given instant. While observing anything in space, time will elapse, and as time elapses, the observed quantum theory will also have moved. In quantum theory, it is the uncertainty principle that cannot determine the precise momentum (time) and position (space) of a particle. In the science of physics, the reductionist philosophy states that any and everything is subatomic energy—from the immense, primeval big bang down to our unseen, fleeting thoughts.

Again, time does not really exist in quantum physics. It exists only as a man-made construct of the human mind. The earth rotates in space in a measureable manner, and we have elected to call this a definition of one day. The earth will continue to rotate, no matter what our concepts are or the terms, names, and definitions we choose to define time with. Consider that the sun never truly rises or sets but only appears to circle the earth. The surface of the earth rotates at one thousand and forty miles per hour. Only from our relative position in time do we believe in a sunset. Picture yourself in outer space, see the larger perspective, and know that it is not the sun that is moving. The sun does not revolve around the earth, but our earth rotates while circling the sun. The earth is traveling through space at 67,108 miles per hour, which is eighty-seven times the speed of sound. The belief that we are sitting still at any given moment is part of a grand illusion. If it were not for gravity, we would surely fly off the face of the earth.

In our minds, we knowingly, or otherwise, tie all of life's activities, events, and even our dreams of the future to the concept of time. We give momentum to our concept of time. The movement of time is not an absolute reality but is a projection of our minds. I can easily recall a moment when time stopped. In the blissful moment of my first kiss with the beautiful woman who was my wife, time seemed to stand still. I had no thought or awareness of either the past or future. No anticipation or trepidation existed at that very moment in the now. The world stood still. This was truly a magical, timeless moment rather than a moment in virtual reality time.

All of the elements of our concept of time are the same phenomena and also occupy space, as in the space-time continuum. Because we cannot experience all of the events of the past, present, and future simultaneously in our minds, we must mentally arrange all events in sequential order of occurrence. In the space-time continuum, space and time are interchangeable and are inversely proportional; more of one is less of the other. Consider an experiment with a car placed upon a one mile runway. Time and space are interwoven interchangeably as the car that is driven the one mile distance (space) at a high rate of speed in a short period of time. Drive the same car very slowly for the same amount of time, and the lesser distance traveled will have been exchanged to accommodate time.

The concepts of space and time challenge our basic beliefs. One of the biggest problems with and stumbling blocks to understanding the causal relationship in our brains is skepticism—or lack of acceptance of the fact that both space and time exist only in our minds. Without time and space, the physical universe disappears. Poof! Only a timeless eternity remains! This possibility sounds scary and unbelievable, but it readily occurs when deep meditation takes us beyond time and space. Also, when we sleep and enter a dream reality, everything appears very real in the dream, even though the experience is not necessarily a familiar environment. And when we awaken from our sleep, the objects and people in the dream disappear. Poof! Consider too that our dreams last from only seconds to as long as twenty minutes. While we dream of events and experiences seeming to last for many hours, the actual wakeful clock time required for the dream is but a fraction of what was perceived while dreaming. In the dream realm, there is no time—only our perception of time after awakening if we recall the dream at all. We awaken from a dream sleep to what we call wakefulness in a virtual reality, and then one day, we will further awaken from this earthly realm to yet another higher realm of wakefulness: a dream within a dream within yet another dream. The Chinese philosopher Zhuang Zhou (369–286 BC) asked this: "Am I a beautiful butterfly dreaming that I am a human, dreaming that I am a butterfly?" With regard to human experience, Zhuang Zhou was neither the butterfly nor the person in his dream; he was simply the conscious experiencer. He was also unknowingly the creator of the entire experience.

There are physicists who believe that there are wormholes in the space-time continuum that might allow time travel. Are these wormholes energy portals changing with the passage of time? Because entropy occurs, I believe that I would not likely wish to travel through time and then not be able to return to my original point because my entry portal had disappeared. Future discoveries in this area of space-time will likely prove to be very exciting.

Our projections of our timely activities are reinforced since our births by our inventions—such as sundials, clocks, and calendars. The development and current use of the very accurate atomic clock is a sophisticated version of measuring time. Also, our relationships with others then depend upon our measurements of so-called time, with scheduled appointments, work hours, vacation days, and the like. Our thinking is done in the now of time, and our activities are scheduled in the past and the future. Our past events in life become part of our unchangeable history. The events of our future, however, exist as possibilities that develop from our dominant thoughts and beliefs. There is also a trap in our creation and use of time. Ask yourself this: "In time, at what age do I think that I am old?" Does the human body come with an expiration date? Do humans die only because we are conditioned to believe that we should not live beyond the community norm of eighty-six years? I prefer to consider the stories of how people in love appear to act and look much younger. Our bodies listen and respond to our beliefs and our thoughts. Even our life's stresses will result in shortening our bodies' cellular telomeres that determine our longevity. Perhaps, we should learn to spend our time wisely, and we should learn who we are and our capabilities. Much depends upon our creative beliefs in order to alter our virtual reality.

Historically, religious scripture, texts, and doctrines have made reference to a secret knowledge, but many of these writing have been changed and rewritten. These scriptures and texts have been passed along to the faithful only after being subjected to interpretation by religious leaders. Many original scriptures and texts available still contain words, phrases, and references written in an esoteric manner. These phrases remain unknown to the average reader. In biblical times, people did not think in terms of energy and thought forms but rather in terms related to the earth and seeds. The secret knowledge is found in one example in Galatians 6:7 (NASB), which says, "For whatsoever a man soweth, that shall he also reap." It was believed that a person's thoughts and actions were the seeds that developed into a person's future, or destiny.

Science has identified the plasma as a vibrating energy field that permeates the entire universe. Our universe is comprised entirely of energy but only 5 percent of it is materialized as physical matter. Recent writings have referred to this creative force as *the Secret*. It is actually the secret knowledge of the ancients that is known as the law of attraction.

When time is spent, eternity begins.

—HELEN HUNT JACKSON

X
The Law of Attraction

Historically, religious scripture, texts, and doctrines have made reference to a secret knowledge, but many of these writings have been changed and rewritten. These scriptures and text have been passed along to the faithful only after being subjected to interpretation by religious leaders. Most of the original scriptures and texts available still contain words, phrases, and references written in an esoteric manner and which remain unknown to the average reader. For example, the verse "And whatever you shall ask in my name, you shall receive" is found in the New American Standard Bible. This esoteric verse does not fully explain what was originally meant. The same is true for this verse: "The kingdom of heaven is within." For centuries, theology stated that prayer was a direct communication with God. Today, the sciences and technology have come to know and understand the truths of the universe and the Universal Law of Attraction that were unavailable to the earliest churches and theologians. Our devout prayers continue to remain a direct link to the creative universe in seeking change in our lives. In previous chapters I have described how our electromagnetic thought energies create a resonance that constructs and governs all matter via molecular movement. This is the basis for the Law of Attraction and the Law of Cause and Effect.

Some people will learn to use the ancient secret knowledge for material gain, while many others will discover and employ the secret knowledge only as a life-changing tool. This tool then hastens our realization of the fact that our human minds—with our beliefs, awareness, and intent—are very powerful. The secret knowledge may become a permanent part of our belief system.

When we decide that we wish to change our beliefs and our destiny, we should consider learning about that secret and esoteric knowledge that has been passed down through the ages—the Law of Attraction. The Law of Attraction has also been referred to as *the secret of the ancients* and is part of the Universal Law of Cause and Effect. This Law of Attraction has been used by many persons known to be incredibly successful throughout their lives. The Law of Attraction is somewhat like the observer effect in that we can consciously manifest or change our physical, emotional, and intellectual realities. Our thoughts, words, and our actions are creative electromagnetic energies. What we conceive, we create, and what we create, we then experience. I believe that most people are not aware that they evoke the Law of Attraction unknowingly and do so hourly. Others do so intentionally. Actually, the Law of Attraction is the entanglement of quantum energy forces at work in a virtual reality. When we accept the creative force of the universe and natural laws, we can use our mind, our imagination, and our willpower to merge with the creative force. We think therefore it is. We are the cause of an effect—we create reality, both physically and via events or experiences.

Our genes do not control or direct our lives as Darwin believed; we do with our consciousness and intent! When we wish to change our environment and our lives, we simply collapse the wave energies involved with our minds with the resulting particle objects. The same may be done with events within our physical view of the universe.

We can learn to live happily within the laws of the universe to manifest material and mental change for transforming our lives. Living within the universal laws provides the basis of intentional living. This is an attractive concept however; we must realize that this can possibly lead us to believe that our minds are controlling our lives. Mentally deciding upon a purpose in life will not necessarily provide a sustainable future. Our existence and our future in this external, physical life are fleeting and subject to random change. A better approach is to know the difference between doing things intentionally and that of just being. For some people, being is living in the present and in the flow of the creative universe. Our true, inner being—a perfect consciousness—is far more beautiful than anything that we could wish to become. The practice of thinking and doing things to fulfill an ever-changing life would be chaotic and lead to frustration, suffering, and a chaotic life. For example, anyone considering acquiring the security of wealth and prestige will find it the equivalent of sitting on a two-legged stool. Intentionally striving to attain or reach a given point or status can preoccupy or dominate one's life yet leave one with only uncertainty or failure. Remember the difference between those things of the mind and those of the heart.

Both our short-term and long-term actions and goals will require that most of our energies be applied to planning for the future, not dwelling on the past. Why not learn to appreciate the present moment, the now? If you think that you can depend upon your thinking alone, just imagine for a moment that your brain is wired to a loudspeaker so your thoughts are broadcasted publicly. You can understand why others might cross the street to avoid you. Our self-talk provides a good example of the extraneous verbiage that often reflects our subconscious beliefs and that can undermine our best intentions. The voice we hear in our heads is the voice of our ego. It is the human ego that loves the idea of having a systematic mental approach to obtaining esteemed levels of sophistication. The human ego will prompt our mind with the capacity to analyze and can only present an intellectual prize to us. Our human awareness and consciousness are not the same as our mental capacity for critical thinking.

Our thoughts and our beliefs are creative energy forms that are sent out into an electromagnetic and ethereal field, and they do not disappear. It is this field that governs particle and wave energies with bosons, which carry the four unified forces of gravity, weak force, strong force, and electromagnetic force. Our thoughts send instant messages to our bodies in ways we could not have imagined. These same energy forms of our thoughts are also sent out into a waiting universe with consequences. This is the Law of Attraction and is part of cause and effect. Simply stated, we cause an effect. Imagine the chaos we cause unknowingly with our random, preoccupied thoughts! Using our mind as a tool allows our thoughts and attitudes to become the keys to changing our cells and attracting a new reality. Recall the four levels of consciousness described by Plato that include the totality of consciousness. When we can experience this highest state of being in awareness, we find a lasting meaning and purpose in accordance with the natural flow of a perfect universe.

Our thoughts leave our minds as energy forms—whether the thought are positive, negative, or neutral. Thought energy can be directed and received, as evidenced in the animal world, with instinctual telepathy. Animals and waterfowl communicate with one another within their respective species using mental telepathy. These communications often have the added force of emotions caused by a sense of danger or fear. For example: both ducks and deer can silently warn their young offspring of impending threats and the need to flee. Another example is the common belief that animals can instinctively sense fear in humans. Dogs have also been trained to indicate when they sense or feel some diseases in humans. These thought energies are never lost. Even our own bodies are listening to our thoughts. When we think negative thoughts, this energy will not only return to us, but it will also attract more of the same or similar energy to us.

How many people live intentionally? Most of us forget our life principles and priorities, and we begin hurrying through life day-to-day, going from place to place, focused upon climbing the next obstacle, closing the next deal, or running a new errand. Consumed by our daily activities, we even become unaware of the levels of our self-talk. We often believe that we never have enough time to accomplish all that we wish to do in our ego-driven activities. We must be careful of what we wish for! We have all the time in the world when we realize that we are the creators of not only time but also this life that we have chosen to experience. Life is then a series of choices, and the choices are ours by intent. Our lives are therefore of our choosing as cocreators. We should do it with intention rather than attract unwanted events and circumstances into our lives with hurried, worried, and random thoughts. If we could throw out all of our unwanted and redundant thoughts, we would then have only memories of happy, loving emotions and emotional experiences.

Knowingly or otherwise, we have been attracting our life events with the energy of our dominant thoughts and beliefs. Do you believe that it was coincidence that you found these pages? Did you have an immediate sense of knowing the truth when you read it? Positive thoughts and beliefs will cause both positive energies and events to be drawn to us and will change our bodies' cells. Knowing this, we can transform our lives with rewarding experiences with a primary purpose in accordance with the universal plan. Our trust and our belief in the process of positive energy attraction are the fundamental elements in making the process work. Some people will call this living in the will of God, while others will call this living in the flow of the creative universe. Remember that we are all components of consciousness, intelligence, energy, and matter within a universe of consciousness!

Everything that we experience in our lives is a result of the vibrations that we have created as energy beings. For centuries, the Law of Attraction has been referred to in esoteric writings and ancient manuscripts, but the scientific community has not yet been able to provide explanations for these phenomena with quantum physics. Many scientists are critical of the Law of Attraction because they believe that if something cannot be documented, repeated, and measured, it cannot exist. Some of the same scientists, however, are continually searching for the God particle.

The Law of Attraction states that like attracts like and that the universe does not pass judgment upon energies or value energy as good, bad, or neutral. With regard to energy, the universe reacts in a precise time frame within the synchronicity of the space-time continuum that interweaves all events. This is how and why our thoughts attract and manifest our experience just as we have thought about the anticipated experience. Our dominant thoughts and beliefs will find a way to manifest in reality because we truly believe in something. In a sense, this is mind over matter. Mind over matter also says that if you don't mind, it won't matter! Our beliefs, desires, expectations, wishes, and even our earnest gratitude hold an immense power. Consider that we have both feelings and thoughts. Typically, our emotional feelings are the stronger of the two. Our emotions can hijack our thoughts and our actions if we are not prepared. All thought energy has polarity. It is positive and negative. Notice I did not say positive *or* negative. Much like light and dark, positive and negative are only opposite ends of the same pole in accordance with the Universal Law of Polarity. When our thoughts are both positive and in alignment with our emotions, they provide an even stronger focus for action. This becomes very important when we consider the use of the Law of Attraction. When coupled with our thoughts and feelings, our words and actions become even more powerful when aligned with our objectives. When our objective is to acquire something, we must focus our thoughts, our feelings, and our verbal wish on the desired response. We must also focus on having something rather than simply wanting it. If we continue to want something, we will be provided with a greater opportunity to further want without having acquired anything. All too often we ask for something without getting what we asked for. When we ask for something or request something to occur or to manifest, we must do so with conviction. As energies go, we already have that which we ask for. The universe cannot tell us no. That which we think about and most desire will be given to us, but only if we truly believe it with conviction. We should then offer fervent and joyous thanks of gratitude. The immense power of prayer is also an example of the Law of Attraction.

The Law of Attraction has often been incorrectly identified with the Law of Cause and Effect. The Law of Attraction works in conjunction with and utilizes the Universal Law of Cause and Effect, the Law of Vibration, the Law of Mentality, and the Law of Rhythm. An old Chinese proverb says, "Life is like an echo, what you send out will return to you." In the biblical sense, the Law of Attraction is said like this: "As you sow, so shall you reap." When we wish to experience something different in our lives, we need to learn to use our vibrational frequencies. If we feel and think well, we will attract more of the things that make us feel good. If we feel badly and think negative things, we will attract even more things and experiences of a similar vibration. Don't worry, be happy!

Realize that your physical reality is not the cause but the effect. We cannot manipulate the effect, but we can change the cause and thereby create the effect. Creating our reality with our thoughts, words, and actions is that simple. Do not succumb to the ancient belief that we have to earn something in order to enjoy it. We do not have to earn anything. It is already there for the asking. In Mark 11:24 (NASB), Jesus was quoted as saying this: "Therefore I say unto you, all things whatsoever ye pray and ask for, believe that ye shall receive them, and you shall have them." Let our thoughts be constructive, and let our sincere requests indicate that we truly believe with conviction that which we ask.

For centuries, the Law of Attraction has been called *the secret knowledge*. It is no longer a secret but is still not understood and lived by many people. The Law of Attraction is not difficult to understand when the timing is right for people who wish to investigate the ancient secret. When we realize that the entire universe is comprised of energy, including even our thoughts, it becomes much easier to understand the phenomena of the Law of Attraction. The creative power of our thoughts manifests everything that we see. Our consciousness is primary, and our reality is secondary and created by our egos, or the human mind. Our potential is limited only by our beliefs. We add meaning and form to everything with our interpretation of other energies. Our beliefs, our thoughts, and our emotions create a powerful energy that attracts those things that we desire to become part of our realities. Learn to choose your beliefs and to abandon those beliefs that do not reflect your wishes or intentions.

Laws are generally promulgated for compliance. If we decide to live by and use the Law of Attraction, we must also obey the same law. To live by the Law of Attraction, we must employ very simple but exact principles. The precise Law of Attraction requires the following actions:

1. Desire. Think enthusiastically about what it is that you desire. Prioritize your values, and be careful about what you ask for. Keep all of your thoughts, feelings, and visualizations positive and enthusiastic in nature. Your thoughts must match your feelings, and the feelings of happiness and joy are very powerful and will intensify your creative energies.
2. Decide. Know, and decide specifically what you wish for. Include your ownership and responsibility for this happening or desired object. Without any doubt, see that it already exists and that you own it as one of multiple possibilities. Your beliefs, intentions, and decisions are creative energies.
3. Ask. Ask very specifically for what you wish to occur. Choose your course of action rather than simply wanting it. Include a reasonable time frame, specific details, and amounts of tangible items. Your request may also be vocalized, but it is your dominant thoughts and beliefs that will manifest the change. Vocalizing your request increases the power of the energies involved.

4. Believe. Believe, as a matter of law, that your request will be manifested because you are a living part of the universal flow. God and the universe want you to be happy, and you owe it to yourself. Also, you should believe and trust in yourself and your capabilities. Success requires that you believe without any doubt that the Law of Attraction will work for you. The slightest subconscious doubt will negate any request that you make.
5. Work. Work the request into your mind daily in a positive manner and with enthusiasm. Imagine, and visualize your request. In a convenient place, post photos, drawings, or other graphic depictions of any physical items that remind you of the request. You should also imagine these items in your hand, your home, your garage, or other locations. Also imagine your thought energies going out onto the ether as particles or waves of information.
6. Express. Think, and say, "Thank you, God" or "Thank you, Universe." As you think and say thank you, genuinely feel the gratitude for the response to your request. With time, you can also say thanks for being reintegrated into the universal flow of things. Your sincere gratitude is a very powerful energy, and it magnifies your intentions.

When using the Law of Attraction, we cannot ask for something not to occur or ask for anything that would be injurious to others. For example, we cannot ask for a better life because this request affirms a negative element that says that we presently have an undesirable or unwanted life. The negative aspect of this request will only attract more of the same negativity to our lives. We can begin by realizing that we already have a good life and that we simply wish to make changes to our lives.

Secondly, our request for something must be reasonable, and we must believe with total faith that what we requested will occur as a matter of absolute law (cause and effect). We may request something to occur within a specified and reasonable time frame, but we will not know the exact timing of the occurrence of our request any more than we can possibly know of the many intricate, interwoven coincidences required to make it happen. We should not even think about how it will happen, as any doubt will negate the request.

A word of caution is advised for anyone creating his or her reality to include valued physical possessions: be very careful in manifesting possessions. These attachments will possess you.

Having now described how to request something from God, or the universe, remember that it is actually you making a request of your higher self in a responsive universe. Many people know and use the Law of Attraction as an integral part of their subjective reality. Others too call it their life of intention. Remember that your reality is created on a need-to-exist basis.

The only true gift is a portion of yourself.

—HOMER

XI

Subjective or Objective Reality

The concept of a subjective reality holds that a belief system is one in which there is only one consciousness and that each of us is that consciousness. This closely relates to the weak anthropic principle that posits that there are no observations without an observer. Observers are necessary to bring the universe into existence. Matter depends upon the concepts of time and space to exist and time and space are not absolute realities but are creations of our human minds. With our minds at the center of creation, we are then the center of our universe.

As sentient beings, our consciousness is a subjective experience. Made in the image of the universe, we are actually God's consciousness. As creative individuals, each of us is the center of our own universe. Anything and everything in our reality are simply projections of our thoughts and beliefs; we have created everything with the permission of the universe. Our physical world is simply that of illusion. Consider for a moment that when you are asleep and dreaming, you create all of the people and the circumstances of your dream. You can do whatever you wish in the context of the dream. It is a combination of our experiences, beliefs, imaginations, and intentions that create the subjective dream. The same is true when we awaken from sleep and our dreams. Our thoughts and our beliefs continue to create our reality. The only universe that exists is the one that is believed to be observed. From countless possibilities, our beliefs and our thoughts create the probability factor that converts to actuality—or reality. And when our physical bodies die, we shall again awaken to a new reality!

A subjective, conscious experience is called *qualia*. Examples might include things tasted, being startled by an unseen gunshot, or the touching a kitten's soft fur. Both real and imagined sensory events are subjective, conscious experiences. Imagine for a moment that you are instructing a blind person in what the star-filled universe looks like. Because the blind person has never observed the nighttime skies, he or she must imagine what you are describing. Is this blind individual not then creating a subjective experience within his or her head? This same person can then picture in his or her mind a changing visual experience of the universe as well. And what then is real? Our thoughts are also a creative energy. Quantum mechanics provides for multiple, simultaneous events and unlimited possibilities. Science is now finding that our human brains are continually conducting multiple and simultaneous quantum computations from the millions of bits of information received per second. From limitless possibilities, we plan and choose our actionable realities.

All truth as we know or experience it is subjective. There is no single, absolute truth, as religions would have us believe. We have only our own individual, separate, and changing views. We also share information with one another and exchange viewpoints and opinions, but we continue to create our individual reality with our private beliefs and dominant thoughts.

With our thoughts, beliefs, and emotions, we create events and scenarios and then actively participate in them. This activity is very much like Geoffrey Chaucer's writing in *The Canterbury Tales* in the fourteenth century. He inserted himself into the story as a character and fellow traveler. Chaucer became part of his own story. Chaucer even described himself in the novel as having poorly written a verse. Similarly, we have also written our present-day scripts and realities with our past dominant thoughts, desires, and beliefs. We provide meaning and value to everything that exists in our reality just for the experience. Knowing this, we can take control and change our reality and our destiny. Yes, we can make our dreams come true. We need only to know our capabilities, our beliefs, and ourselves. The stronger our belief in our capabilities the more frequently our dreams come to life! Further investigation and experimentation will show us that our world is an illusion created only in our minds.

In 1919, scientists Theodore Kaluza and Oscar Klein determined the theory of numerous spatial dimensions beyond the three then known. The notable physicist Werner Heisenberg later realized the duality of wave and particle energy in nature with the uncertainty in predicting, measuring, and knowing the mass (position) and velocity (momentum) of energies. The futures of energy and nature cannot be determined because energy is constantly moving, and this implies the fourth spatial element of time. Once past a certain point in time, energy can never return. Reality is not created from outside of ourselves, but from the inside outwardly. Our mind is the creative matrix. Likewise, our concept of time is created from the inside out. For too long the world has been developing the wrong rules for our game of life with the materialistic view of an objective reality. Wrong rules will produce the wrong outcome.

Objective reality exists independently of the human mind, whereas subjective reality is dependent upon the mind for existence. A dictionary definition of *objective reality* is "perceiving reality, all that confronts our awareness, as it is." It is a matter of seeing things as they are rather than seeing things from a certain point of view or position. Objectivity supposes that all events and objects in creation already exist and that we all see events and objects in the same way. We do observe physical objects the same way as others because of entanglement, but there is a difference in how each of us perceives them. It all depends upon your perception, awareness, or point of view. Apparently, at times, we have both subjective and objective elements in our perceived reality. When a baby is born, the infant is not likely to be aware of his or her awareness and will experience an objective reality. The infant has not yet acquired the experience to give meaning or value to anything. Imagine then that we continue on from infancy through life with a perception of an objective reality. Our objective reality may or may not change to that of a subjective reality dependent upon our knowledge and awareness. As we grow in experience, we grow in awareness and develop, or create meaning and values by which we observe and judge new experiences.

In quantum physics, there is the physical phenomenon of entanglement. In this phenomenon, pairs or groups of particles are generated and then combine and interact together so that their quantum states cannot be described independently. A person with objective perception will still unknowingly generate particle matter and view the very same physical objects that another person perceives subjectively. They will both see the same object, but only one of them will know how it was created. Again, this all depends upon our awareness and intention. This may be further complicated by the locality and nonlocality issues in physics. Locality states that an object is influenced directly by its immediate surroundings. Nonlocality allows that an object may be influenced by another object, even though the objects are separated in space with no perceivable intermediate mechanism. There is nothing found in quantum physics to deny entanglement. Our perceived particle objects may merge with those of persons in another part of the world without regard to time or space.

There is another aspect of quantum physics called *superposition*. Theoretical physics has demonstrated in a small scale experiment that particle energies can exist in separate states of superposition at the same time until they are observed, disturbed, or otherwise impacted by their surroundings. Particle (matter) energies may then collapse and return to wave energy properties. First you see it, poof, and then you don't! Even human thought energies can change or disturb other superposition particles of the phenomenon being observed—hence, the observer effect.

The Freudian theory in psychology says that each of us has a three-part identity at birth—the id, the ego, and the superego. The id describes our instinctual drives, such as fear, love, anger, and hunger. The id opposes our moral superegos. The human ego then moderates our behavioral choices between the id and the superego. Psychology further suggests that these are the three faces of reality that each of us lives with. There are our perceived realities, which are known only to each of us; another face that we present to others; and a third reality of that which others see in each of us. From birth until physical death, our realities continue to change and evolve. We also develop our volition, or free will. When we become aware of the difference between objective reality and subjective reality, we then use the law of attraction to further create and expand our subjective reality. We can then create our experience. Do you know what has been your experience? Stop, and consider the consequences of your past thoughts, decisions, actions. Consider the multiple alternative possibilities.

We routinely use the Law of Attraction to acquire our experiences, whether knowingly or otherwise. There have been many times when I have asked for a heavy rain to stop momentarily until I could get indoors and graciously said my thanks when it happened. Have you ever asked for an open parking space in a crowded parking lot and have it appear immediately? Can you recall the times that you have thought about a distant friend only to have that friend suddenly phone you or write to you? I would bet that many of us have, at one time or another, said, "God, get me through this, and I will never do it again." And once again, we got through another crisis by way of a miracle. Oftentimes, we are amazed by an unexpected, coincidental happening, which is yet another possibility. The real miracle occurs when all other life's miracles are no longer seen as such but as a matter of our intent. The creative source of these miracles is a remarkable element of life's processes. Because of cause and effect, the greatest miracle of all is that of our created reality. A second great miracle occurs at the moment of our physical death and we instantly see and know the entire scheme of creation and levels of experienced reality.

Many years ago, I once stepped up to the tee with my golf club and announced matter-of-factly to the others in my foursome that I was about to shoot a 185-yard hole in one. At this age in my life, I could only occasionally break one hundred on a golf course. My prediction was met with a lot of friendly laughter, but on this day, I was a confident, amateur seventeen-year-old boy. I teed the ball and began my swing. Even before I hit the ball with my club, I knew that the golf ball was headed for the hole on the distant green. With that one shot, I became the most talked about "pro" for the next week. Was this a miracle? For me, the true miracle was not the experience of knowing in advance that I would make the hole in one and doing it. The entire incident was but a small part of my miraculous life created by my dominant beliefs and thoughts.

There is a distinct difference between making a wish and hoping that it might occur and requesting an action with the faith and conviction that it will occur with certainty. We need only to learn to manage the wave and particle energies in our lives. And when our knowledgeable faith is strong, and when we firmly believe in the Law of Attraction, our requests are answered quickly. When we make a request for something, we cannot for a moment try to begin to understand how it will happen. There may be hundreds of coincidental factors occurring behind the scenes, and our questioning will only cause doubt. A continuing confidence and belief in one's self will cause doubt to be replaced by an emotional enthusiasm that coalesces with one's thoughts in a powerful way. The more often our requests are answered, the stronger our faith then becomes, and it is reciprocal.

Some believe that there are possibly even more dimensions yet unknown to us. Why not? Every changing moment in time contains the possibilities of multiple events or experiences. Events and material objects are simply static particle and wave energy possibilities awaiting a change or disturbance to influence the energy form. Many people believe that because an unlimited number of dimensions are available, it is we, the human observers that determine or choose any one of the multiple possibilities solely because of our consciousness and the energies of our beliefs, awareness and thoughts. All of the aspects of our daily reality are existent in the universe, just waiting for our awareness to add meaning and value to our human experience. All people do not experience space and time, as measured in distance and duration, identically. When we choose from what is known to us, we are choosing from our egos' information, and we will likely experience familiar, comfortable, but sometimes even unwanted, random experiences. When we realize that we are pure consciousness, we will become aware that we have multiple possibilities from which to choose. We can then choose to grow in happiness, love, beauty, truth, and peace.

There are other interesting phenomena involved with our thought energies. One example has shown that the fifth classical element of the ether has a time delay. When we make repeated visualizations and requests for something, the repetition is the equivalent of repeated strikes of a hammer upon a solid object. The repeated request is then accelerated proportionately. It has also been demonstrated that a concentrated meditation of a group of several persons creates a powerful energy to promote material and behavioral change. We create not only our physical realities but also events or occurrences in our current lives and our tomorrows. Our rapidly evolving humanity is propelled by the power of a collective consciousness.

Some physicists and others, including myself, believe that the choices and requests that we make will necessarily commingle and integrate with those of countless others in a synchronistic manner. Quantum mechanics calls this phenomenon *entanglement*. Physicists have added the element of the human experience to their theories in order to validate and complete the space-time continuum. I choose to substitute the word *awareness* for the physicists' term of experience.

Simply stated, we create our own reality, and we do so with our awareness, beliefs, thoughts, and volition. Our developing of multisensory perception will facilitate creating reality. Remember that when we change the way in which we see things, we will change the things that we see.

Throughout this writing, I have discussed the concept of coincidence. The correct word for coincidence is *synchronicity*. Synchronicity is provided by the continuous ebb and flow of our energetic universe. It has also been said that coincidence is the whisper of God, the creative universe. The unexpected and unique events that we often experience and think of as coincidental are the synchronicity of our universe. It is synchronicity that provides the manifestation and delivery of those things that we have requested of the universe. Coincidence plays such an important role in our lives, and yet many people do not recognize or understand the phenomenon. Some will say that there is no such thing as coincidence because all things in our lives are preordained as necessary for the overall integration of our affairs. Nevertheless, these events must still coincide. We should learn to see the beauty in the synchronicity and the exquisite timing of the many events interwoven into our lives. When we truly know and recognize the manner in which synchronicity prevails, we can align our mentality and our daily activities to coincide with the universal flow of energy and events. The 1960s popular expression was "go with the flow." This saying holds true today as well.

Closely related to synchronicity is the element of our human consciousness called *intuition*. Intuition is the very subtle feeling of knowing that comes to us as a gut feeling or as something we just knew intuitively. When synchronicity brings us to a fork in the road for decisions, we should be aware of and follow our intuition rather than the unreliable reasoning of our minds. All too often the human mind and ego will lead us to a lesser choice.

When we are fully aware of its source, intuition is more easily understood. Human intuition most often arrives quickly, coming from the subconscious level of our awareness to our cognitive awareness. This intuition cannot be developed but is simply there. We can, however, learn to recognize the intuitive thoughts brought to our awareness and develop our responses accordingly. With continued use of our intuition, it will increase in occurrence as a universal guide. It is the rational, thinking function of the human mind that will alter, destroy, or recognize a bit of information that we intuitively know to be true without having previously thought about it. When we are presented with a coincidence or a series of coincidences, it is our intuition that first brings our awareness into focus. Incredibly, after we recognize the synchronicity of events, more coincidences will follow unexpectedly and will be unscheduled. Our human intuition will make the right choice and decision every time in the flow of the universe. Some have said that coincidence is the universe's prompting and showing us the way. Because our intuition is always correct, I tend to believe that our intuition is somehow related to or based upon the akashic field of the total knowledge of all that ever was and is. It is intuition that reminds us, warns us, and advises us of the correctness and truthfulness in all matters.

> *Love puts the music in laughter, the beauty in song, the warmth in a shoulder, the gentle in strong…*
> *Love puts the magic in memories, the sunshine in skies, the gladness in giving, the starlight in eyes…*
> *Love puts the fun in together, the sad in apart, the hope in tomorrow, the joy in a heart.*
>
> —ANONYMOUS

XII

Meditation and Mindfulness

Many people consider themselves as seekers of the ultimate truth and enlightenment via meditation. Very likely, most of these people are unaware that what they seek, they already are. Our reality includes a tangled assortment of various experiences. That which they are attempting to find is the experiencer who is ever-present no matter the experience.

Meditation techniques can reveal higher levels or realms of consciousness, but it is difficult to find the words to adequately describe these experiences that are beyond causation in the space and time dimensions. In meditation we can leave the realm of the mind and experience the wonders of the heart. The higher realms of experience do not need a phonetic language or a construct of measurable time. Recall Plato's description of consciousness and reality as having four levels—from fantasy and illusion to sensual awareness to reasoning and knowledge to total consciousness. In a previous chapter I described how our mental requirement for time can be slowed and stopped in the present, or the now of time. From within the position of the now, we can escape the human mind's requirement for time, and those millions of data per second are not required to process information. We are then in a timeless and total awareness—and consciousness without thought.

We should also consider the fact that some people have a great deal of difficulty in reaching a deep meditative state of awareness. For many, the practice of a deep, profound, and directed contemplation can be equally beneficial. Both meditation and contemplative prayer may be done for many purposes, and both can raise our human awareness beyond our bodily senses and reasoning and allow us the life-changing experience of the totality of consciousness. Both our history and our future illustrate our evolving, increasing consciousness. True enlightenment is not found in words and material pursuits but in the silence of the body- temple of meditation.

Meditation is not for everyone. Many people believe that meditation is a necessary religious and spiritual practice to actualize the higher self. Whether spiritual or not, meditation provides many life-changing benefits with physical, mental, or intellectual change. Anyone deciding to do meditation should select the type of meditation and technique needed for a specific result or benefit. There are also several forms or techniques of meditation used solely for relaxation and medical healing modalities. A word of caution is advised in selecting a meditative technique to establish a continued practice just for the sake of meditating. For example, to establish a meditation ritual at a certain time of day in a specific position and location is nothing more than a ritual of doing rather than that of simply being in the present, relaxing moment. There is little or no benefit to meditating with the attitude of pride in achievement or in meditating only because someone instructed you to do so. Far too many people readily acclaim their mental and physical disciplines for sitting in structured daily meditation at certain times. True happiness, peace, inner self-awareness, and health do not depend upon pride or self-imposed rituals.

For the uninitiated, try to imagine sitting in meditation with closed eyes and an intense concentration on the words and activity of the mind. In this method, we can lose all awareness of the bodily senses and concentrate on the incessant chattering of the mind.

With complete attention directed to the activity of the mind, we can become completely unaware of our physical bodies. Some meditative techniques strive to silence the chatter of the mind, while others strive to control and direct the chatter. With practice and experience, we can even silence the chattering mind and move to other levels of consciousness. It is the human mind that requires time and space in which to operate. There are several techniques available to quiet the mind and lead one to a higher and more transcendent level of consciousness beyond time and space. Meditation can also provide catharsis in that our complex human problems may be instantly brought into total conscious awareness and understanding. At the higher levels of consciousness, we can receive instant messages or knowledge and understanding without phonetic content of matters not previously known.

When we leave the physical world of our bodily senses and enter the inner realm through meditation, we abandon space and time to be in the now. From a previous chapter, recall the differentiation shown between our physical body and that of our spiritual body—or soul, often called our higher self. Intentional meditation provides the opportunity for our spiritual bodies to coalesce with our physical bodies in the now of time. In her book *Love without End*, Glenda Green has written that there is a point within each of us where the physical, emotional, intellectual, spiritual, and intentional elements of our existence are in perfect synchronicity—a perfect zero point. This occurrence is experienced prior to our birth, immediately after death, and at any other time that our will is in sync with the will of the creative universe, or God. This is the very same energy zero point—the vacuum base that includes all the energy fields described in earlier chapters. Others have described this realm as providing a communion with God and a supernatural peace beyond understanding or description. Several religious movements have described this meditative state as having the power to open the tenth gate to spiritual enlightenment and the door to God's house. This phenomenon is also described as the blossoming of a many-petaled lotus flower.

Several types of meditation include the more popular ones described here:

Guided meditation is guided imagery or visualization. We can form mental images of places and situations that are relaxing. This is often done with a guide or instructor who can prompt new images and a recall of our pleasant visual experiences from our memories. Guided meditation can be very helpful in finding relaxation in our bodies and our minds, and it offers health and medical benefits, such as lowered blood pressure and heart rate. Guided meditation allows us to put aside and forget the day's stresses with relaxation as a substitute.

Mantra meditation involves the repetition of a word or phrase, either silently or aloud, to ward off distracting thoughts in achieving stillness of mind and body. Because the human mind is capable of many simultaneous communications channels, it may be very difficult to silence the incessant chattering of the mind. When we attempt to silence or occupy one channel, the human mind will open yet another channel to accommodate separate chatter or dialogue. The use of a phonetic mantra may be used then to concentrate or focus our attention or to clear our minds. Oftentimes, a meaningless, undefined word or a short string of words may be used to concentrate human attention, as this uncommon word will not require examination by the inquisitive mind. A very popular mantra is the name *Lord* or any other name of a beloved individual.

Classical yoga—described as union of the body, mind, and spirit—includes physical posturing with mental concentration in order to reach a spiritual union with the divine. In Hindu philosophy, bhakti yoga includes a deep meditation to reach a realization of and surrender to God.

Bhakti yoga is the Hindu philosophy and devotional yogic worship, with the acts of love, faith, and surrender to God. Bhakti yoga is often described as developing a personal relationship with God to find the divinity within one's self through the heart center.

Mindfulness meditation is very popular and is used to increase our awareness. It focuses on living in the present moment. We can concentrate on that which we are experiencing in the meditation or concentrate our attention on a special event or past experience. Some people often begin by concentrating and listening to their breathing and relaxation, while others choose to dwell upon meaningful and joyous past happenings. Mindful meditation may also provide an intense, acute awareness of our emotions and dominant thoughts. I have found that when I can clear my mind of my daily activity and any unresolved issues, often a new passage or book chapter will come into my awareness. Sometimes, clarification is given to me for an unsettled issue on my mind. This messaging also occurs during my restful nighttime episodes and lucid dreams, and I awaken for the day with a new experience and with new information to conduct further research for my writing.

Movement meditation teaches us to focus on our breathing while performing slow, fluid movements—such as walking, tai chi, and qigong. Our physical and mental limitations will often limit our meditation techniques. It has been documented that meditation may extend our life expectancies and that the practice of deep meditation can open the mind to an immense source of previously unknown information, knowledge, and understanding that lie beyond space, time, and phonetic language.

Contemplative prayer is a meditative practice thought to have originated with fourth-century Christian monks who were influenced by Buddhist and Zen practices. This silent meditation asks the practitioner to close his or her eyes and become aware of all superficial thoughts and to concentrate on love and his or her intention to silence the mind. In this manner one can experience only the abundant love within the universe. This is the unknowing of all things in order to find divinity within the self. This is also the zero point wherein our spiritual, physical, emotional, and intentional existence comes into sync in an awesome silence. This is my favorite meditation because of the emotional intensity and the results acquired involve the total body, mind, heart, and soul. After seventy-six years, I have discovered how little I really know.

There are local contemplative centers and organizations that provide study and instruction in contemplative prayer. Contemplative meditation includes the belief that there are five basic levels of contemplative development that culminate in contemplative prayer. These five stages represent levels of moral and spiritual development. The age ranges and numbers of people involved in meditation remain variable because of the constantly changing society in evolutionary growth.

The first stage includes that of humans from birth to approximately fifteen years of age. During this stage, most humans are most likely to be self-oriented and consumed with their rapid physical and emotional growth as well as hormonal issues. For many teenagers, increased awareness, religion, or communion with God is not a priority.

The next stage is from age fifteen to approximately age thirty-five and includes those persons searching for meaning and purpose in their lives and who are contemplating which path will provide a moral compass. Others may reject all aspects of religion. Within this second stage, adults will continue to struggle with decisions and judgments relative to what is good, bad, improper, and verifiably true. As they mature, these persons will explore and begin to select and validate their choices of religious beliefs and knowledge. Unfortunately, some of these persons will continue forever at this level because of their mental approaches without a satisfying experience of the heart.

The third stage is from approximately age thirty-five to fifty-five and probably includes a majority of persons who have decided upon their own respective philosophies and religious beliefs. These people further believe that their path is the only true path, having contemplated others at length. However, many of these folks will surrender to doubt and dissatisfaction and return to stage two to continue searching for definitive and satisfactory answers.

The fourth stage of contemplative development includes people of fifty-five years of age and older—people who have matured with open minds and loving hearts and that now allow that all religious beliefs share a commonality and similar origins. They further believe that there is no right or wrong religion but that all religions are likely necessary for human development and spiritual enlightenment. It is believed that these people have engaged in and benefitted from the deeply profound method of contemplative prayer—not from the process itself but from the resulting surrender to divine love. Certainly, these folks have found an increased awareness, expanded consciousness, and a measure of enlightening. A personal peace and life purpose will also be theirs. Many will also find answers about their true identity, or higher self.

In addition to contemplative prayer, many other forms of meditation are also forms of prayer and communion with God. The power of prayer is a very common theme or expression; however, many people do not fully understand the truly great manifest power contained within prayer. A sincere, devoted prayer is often a form of meditation. Taken a step further, meditation may be made actionable and expanded beyond a limited experience of a few hours. In time and with practice, meditation can include all of our daily activities when our minds and hearts are in the right place. This advanced practice is called *living meditation*. Practiced daily, our relationships with others and our human experience will be uplifting and fulfilling.

In his book *The Elegant Universe*, author and physicist Brian Greene asks this question: "Was there a period in our cosmology that the universe was without the notion of time and space?" When we learn to reach a higher realm beyond time and space in meditation, we realize that there is a timeless state of pure consciousness. Only in the human mind do we create the space-time continuum of a visible universe. Our true being is that of pure consciousness, and consciousness cannot be destroyed. It can only be expressed as experience. One day, Brian Greene will experience an eternity beyond time.

All of the elements of consciousness and human awareness are sometimes taken for granted in constructing the "I" of our identities. This can only result in a duality or separation of the experiencer from the experience. The human experience provides for conscious states beyond the mind, words, ideas, concepts, and yes, also books. This experience is not reserved for enlightened gurus and masters. We need only to go within the human body temple to escape the duality of the "I."

Many people believe that our consciousness is *just there* and that we cannot change our consciousness. Others know that we can alter or raise our own consciousness, or state of being, with an increased awareness. If we are simply coasting through life without control and intention, our consciousness and deep beliefs will create and influence our life experiences. Without intent and commitment this does not provide change, growth, or spiritual transformation. Our past experiences and the beliefs programmed into our consciousness will be retrieved to create even more of the same kinds of random, unwanted experiences. Stuck in the past, our beliefs, thoughts, habits, and actions will not provide a change in our values or our destinies. It is important to know and understand that we have the capability to use our awareness and to step outside of our consciousness and realize what has been happening. We also have the capability to create our individual realities and the experiences that we desire. Evolutionary theory has now been shown not to be random. We are not a Darwinian race of the fittest. Our evolution can now include a collective effort to change societal beliefs and behaviors at a national and international level.

> *People take different roads seeking fulfillment and happiness. Just because they're not on your road doesn't mean that they've gotten lost.*
>
> —Dalai Lama

XIII

Body, Mind and Spirit

In the realm of physics, a critical mass is the smallest mass of a fissionable material that will sustain a nuclear chain reaction at a constant level. The term *critical mass* is also often used to describe other events and activities. I have used the term for the purpose of our discussion relative to an evolving and planetary population. Life as we know it is changing. Worldwide, the growing critical mass of people will reach the minimum number of people necessary for a sustainable action by the majority in prompting our transformation. We are forging an epic change in the nature of humanity to coincide with a changing global consciousness. Our beliefs are creative energy and are relevant to modern life.

For many people, the current world state of affairs can appear an unhappy chaotic mess. Perhaps we have been participants in changing a collective consciousness? We must ask ourselves, "What part, if any, did we play in creating such chaos or crisis? Did we add energy to these conditions? And what can we do as individuals to join the cause for change?" Our individual evolutionary growth will impact others within our sphere of contacts and influence. The conflict that we see and experience is often the result of the collective consciousness of our planet. Knowingly or otherwise, each of us has contributed to the global chaos with our creative thoughts, attitudes, actions, and even our inactions. To do nothing is also a decision. We make real that which we give our attention and energy.

When taken to the extreme, our beliefs can include both rational and irrational concepts regarding social values of life and culture. An ideology is an imaginary relationship of unconscious and conscious beliefs, ideas, ideals, and expectations in the perceived and real-world existence. Ideologies formed from beliefs are the basis of economic, political, and religious theory and policy.

There are no contradictions and no right and wrong in our perfect universe. Everything is in a required balance, and our experiences of things and events happen for a reason. We can't always know the reasons; however, everything works out to completion, though not always to our liking. Today, there are the events of economic crisis, civil unrest, political upheaval, societal breakdown, intractable global violence and conflict, and an absence of spirituality. Opposing religious beliefs and practices have led to radical ideologies and religious movements. There are still countries with religions and customs that mandate beheadings, the cutting off of noses and hands, and other barbaric practices to control the behaviors of others for religious or ideological reasons. Truly, this is not a happy, loving scenario.

It becomes easier to understand why Darwin incorrectly believed that our genes were responsible for the survival of the fittest. The truth of the matter is that our fight or flight survival responses are no longer necessary for our survival. We have learned that a very large percentage of the world's problems are caused by our relationships with one another and by opposing religious cultures and beliefs. We have been killing each other for centuries and not because of politics, economics, or military conquests but because of differing views of religion and a lack of spirituality and civility.

We are also destroying our planet in many ways. It is becoming increasingly evident that the major institutions of our world communities are, for the first time in recorded history, simultaneously collapsing or being destroyed. Think of each of the major institutions—such as education, health, finance, government, commerce, religion, arts, agriculture, theater, and so forth—and observe the rapid rate of deterioration occurring globally. Obviously, some civilizations are more evolved than others—not only in technology, medicine, and the arts but also in their laws and customs. When some cultures learn, grow, and evolve, they find a balance between the ancient duality of spirituality versus materialism. Other cultures cease to learn and grow and fail to evolve. Some cultures respond to their limited beliefs and customs because of radicalized religious beliefs. These same underdeveloped cultures will take advantage of technological advances in other cultures but will hold fast to ancient or outmoded beliefs. Some beliefs can become dangerous self-fulfilling ideologies.

It is ironic that religion seems to be a continuing source of conflict between peoples and nations and a hindrance to a peaceful evolution. Today's religious movements and beliefs continue to promote comparisons and competition between churches and the faithful. As evident today, a global threat of terrorism by radical Muslims has caused many civilizations to experience fear and a resulting discrimination and prejudice. The true moral authority is acquired through suasion rather than by force of religious doctrine, dogma, violence, or law. We must seek the higher moral levels of our natural divinity.

Our current age is also one of transition, and loving, spiritual partnerships are now needed. For too long, our world's population has been exposed to outdated beliefs, customs, and competitive practices that only reinforce or foster more of the same old ways of competition, power, control, greed, and fear. Even our customs, laws, physical structures, and institutional beliefs hold us hostage to outdated beliefs and values. Remember that beliefs, thoughts, and values will shape all of our behaviors as well as our world.

A new world order that prioritizes self-realization will provide purpose, meaning, and worth to our lives devoid of power struggles and human subjugation. Our personal benefits will include a profound sense of peace, joy, comfort, and an age of enlightenment.

This will require a major shift in priorities to necessitate changes in all of our major institutions—such as government, education, religion, commerce, and so on. The power of our collective beliefs can create and change societal institutions.

Our consciousness is primary and is the basis and cause for all human life. It is very important to know and define our life principles in our virtual reality. What is it that we believe in rather than against? We can create a different future while there is still time! Because our beliefs will determine our intentions and actions, we can knowingly use these abilities to create change. In a quantum universe, there is nothing solid or fixed. Our world is full of limitless possibilities that are waiting to be actualized by our intent. Using the creative capabilities of our minds and our consciousness, we can individually make the transformational changes to that which we see in our reality!

Our evolutionary imperatives require the global growth of biological communities—much like our individual cellular biological communities of bodily organs. Think of the human body as a collection of particles of matter in the universal field. Within our physical bodies, there is more space between particles than there is matter. Consider then that our spacey bodies are but specks in the unified energy field. Because matter is never lost or destroyed, our particle bodies are comprised of previously used matter. This should give us pause to think about how we are all related to one another on this earth; we are a continually changing community of particle matter.

In a quantum universe, there is nothing solid or fixed. Over the years, we have lost our sense of community in more ways than one. Much like the microscopic cells of our bodies, we are all part of a large community of miniscule elements that make up our planet and our universe. In this sense, all people of this world are of one source and identity. If you consider the world an integrated global community, you will see that a crisis in one nation has an effect on all others. We must all work cooperatively and in unison to provide solutions to all of the crises in our major institutions. There is an emerging belief and world view that a coming fundamental shift in the global consciousness will profoundly change the very nature of humankind.

The evolution of collective consciousness of humankind is causing the fundamental shift in human nature. Our transformative change will continue to be slow until the scientists, clergypersons, and medical professionals begin to abandon the ancient precepts and standards. The outdated standards, rules, practices, and beliefs are limited in not including consciousness in their respective life roles, activities, and studies.

So how can one person make a difference in this world? Although we are individually but one among millions, we need not feel overwhelmed. We can recognize our personal responsibility, and change will begin with one person at a time adding to a growing awareness until we reach a point of critical mass. The faster that evolutionary change occurs, the sooner we will reach an event horizon in time. At that point, the critical mass cannot be stopped or reversed. It would be the end of this troubled world as we know it!

When we choose to elevate our consciousness, it is immediately raised by our intent. We already are that which we seek. In as much as we create our chaotic reality, we can also create a pleasurable experience to replace it. As interdimensional beings, we came to this earth to use the cosmos as our palette to create our physical and mental reality and to then enjoy it. This is our life, our awareness, and our choice. Why not choose to hasten our evolution to the level of our inherent spirituality and a raised awareness and consciousness? We can choose to form unions of happy, loving hearts and minds.

The worldwide movement or evolution has already begun. Don't get left behind; the critical mass is building. So many people in this country feel, or know intuitively, that something big is about to occur. Life comes at us fast, and many of us feel that the human race is about to take a quantum leap forward in evolutionary development. The rapid acceleration in technology and in the development of physical matter has outpaced our creative capabilities and our understanding of our spiritual decline. Even our genetic process of growth has accelerated. Our biological bodies have evolved and will continue to slowly adjust to our environments. It is the capacity of our minds that must now be explored, understood, and developed to the full human potential. This is the key to the future of our humanity! Exploring our human consciousness will provide a paradigm shift in our consciousness and our growing awareness. Our collective consciousness has already begun to manifest a major shift. This evolution of consciousness will likely include many and various changes in critical areas. We must sooner or later change from exploring our material pursuits to an internal exploration and personal growth, development, and enlightenment.

We have continuously been designing and creating our universe and our reality. We must now take responsibility for our lives and rid ourselves of negative scripts. Our every thought and emotion has a vibratory rate and a positive and negative mode. Listen to the words of our egos coming from our mouths as well as those inside of our heads. We can learn to think and speak affirmatively as our well-being depends upon it. We can think and be proactive, learning not to depend upon unfulfilled hopes and misplaced trust.

We can discover our full human potential as we already have all of the answers within. It is time to do that which we were placed here on earth to do. Using our human will, or volition, we can propel our thoughts across the unified field. We can visualize the change that we wish to make. Because our dominant thoughts reflect our beliefs and create our manifest future, our emotions will further intensify the strength and power of our thought energies. We should know and be aware of our most intimate thoughts and desires and formulate an informed request of the universe. Repeated requests made with complete faith in a positive result will amplify the energy and the force needed for delivery. An attitude of sincere gratitude also strengthens the process. Be, and live the change that you wish to make in the universe. Remember too, that there is no shame in failure, only more opportunity.

Body, mind, and spirit—the human experience! Recall Plato's levels of reality—illusion, the senses, reasoning, and spirituality. Each of our individual worlds or realities is comprised of a body, a mind, and spirit—or consciousness. Each of these three elements has a unique function. What we experience in our physical bodies is simply an effect created by our dominant thoughts and beliefs. The human body is but our experience vehicle and cannot create or cause anything. Our thoughts cannot experience but will create the reality to provide our experience. The spirit is consciousness and is primary. Our human consciousness provides the energy and intelligence for both our thoughts and our bodies. Remember that your primary purpose in this life is to be and to create and to then experience and enjoy your creation. So who are you? And what are your beliefs? Are you satisfied with what you have created of yourself and your human experience? Ask yourself, "Do I live the life I love? And do I love the life I live?" Our human consciousness is but a small part of the much larger expanse of a universal consciousness.

Sometimes our lessons are difficult and repeated until learned by experience. Tragedy, crisis, and calamity are a part of the fabric of our lives and will quickly get our attention. Facilitated by our capacity for memory, strife and sorrow will be remembered very long and will form the basis of those things learned best. For many people, the risk of pain will deny passion. Personal tragedy, loss, and grief can also expand the boundaries and depth of our emotions. To the extent that we know love, we also experience grief and sorrow.

Some believe that critical events in the lives of humans will build character. Other people will not learn and grow but will succumb to despair and a life of failure. Are life's tragedies and tests of our own making? I prefer to think and to believe that life-altering events are brought to us as a matter of balancing cause and effect and that the same roles were preordained by our prior dominant thoughts and beliefs. As we grow in age and experience, the content of our responses to life-changing events becomes less emotionally challenging and more moderate. Once we become aware of this process, we can become proactive in changing our beliefs and our lives rather than simply responding to an unknown and seemingly unpredictable future.

The thirteenth-century poet Jalal Rumi said this: "Let the beauty we love be what we do." The beauty we love is reflected in a meaningful life. The ancient quests for a meaningful life and a life with purpose may be achieved, as these quests directly relate to our beliefs. Our purpose in life is to add meaning to our experiences of life. Life has no meaning until each of us brings definition or meaning to this human life. It is a great misunderstanding to ask for the meaning of life when we are the answer. There is no one grand theme or cosmic plan for all of us. We must individually learn to decide and to choose that which is meaningful to live for. Why not choose to be joyous in achieving self-actualization of mind and body?

Something meaningful will likely be considered to be in accordance with our core beliefs. This individual meaning will be evident when we have an acute awareness of our core beliefs, life principles, values, and those things believed to be self-satisfying. Consider Maslow's theory of human need, which outlines our upward evolution and growth and the search for self-actualization. Then ask yourself this: "Why am I here? Why am I a living being entrusted with volition and will?" A common belief answers many of our questions by explaining that we are here to create experience with meaning and to enjoy our creation. Our purpose in life is to live it, create our individual reality in consciousness, and to enjoy life, love, and joy to the utmost. By creating something to live for, we also create ourselves as conscious, loving, happy beings.

So how do we know with certainty that we have changed our physical, earthly, personal bodies to align with our spiritual souls? As we rise in awareness to the highest levels of self-actualization, we can begin to sense an internal change as our physical, earthly bodies and our souls act as one. The world around us changes—including our activities and our interactions with many others. Our relationships become those of an open, loving heart. People with very expressive attitudes will change others with whom they interact. Our attitudes are formed from our basic core values and beliefs that will become our behavioral displays. Positive or negative, our influential attitudes will evoke physical and emotional changes in others. When we are emotionally and physically happy, positive, cheerful, vibrant, loving, and expressive, we forever change our environments and our life experiences.

We also evolve as global citizens with concerned worldviews. As we grow in knowledge we feel empowered. As our world of experiences evolves, we begin to exist as an expression of our higher selves. Unique as we are individually, there is no particular process for us to achieve self-actualization; however, there are several steps or levels that we will likely experience. To begin, we must truly desire to change our existing realities beyond the realm of our five bodily senses. There are levels of higher awareness to discover with knowledge and perseverance. We will usually have to reconsider the importance of conventional thinking and materialistic values as we experience a new realization.

Our human intuition that comes from within will prove to be a guide for us. A new or changing reality may also require that we begin to live in accordance with our true beliefs as an example for others. Along the path to our new reality, we should look forward to meeting new people and should share ideas, talents, gifts, and learning. As we progress, we will find not only our true identities, but we will also see our purposes and meaning in this earthly theater of which we are the directors.

We can begin by looking at our daily activities and our relationships. Our lives will improve as well as influence those with whom we interact daily. Each of us can be a force for change for those people whose lives are intertwined with ours when we make them more aware of an evolving humanity. Try beginning each day with a positive and grateful thank you. Relax, and realize that we often have much to smile about that we can share.

Our relationships with all others will improve dramatically when we engage them with direct eye contact and hold that eye contact unashamedly while interacting. Smile often, even for no particular reason, with others. Smiling promotes the human connection of love. When possible and appropriate, share a hug with others to insure a mutual and loving trust. The value of physical contact for humans is well documented medically. Each of us needs the occasional touch of another human. When appropriate, a gentle touch on the hand, arm, or shoulder of another is both reassuring and builds trust and acceptance. The exchange of vibrational energies will change everyone involved in positive ways. Those we know, love, and live with will eventually come to love their entire creation as we do.

We are entering a new era of personal and global enlightenment and raised consciousness. An evolutionary moment of truth has arrived, and the consequences of the rapid acceleration in evolution will likely create problems with global ramifications not previously experienced. In past years and centuries, societal change occurred very slowly. Now, countries, nations, cities, and families are rapidly developing—some more slowing than others—causing disparities and conflict. Our physical, mental, emotional, and spiritual realities are in revolutionary changes.

However, there are things we can learn from social transformation. Our world of competition will change to that of cooperation. We can change one day at a time and one person at a time. We can redefine our lives by living the truths that we know and believe. We can significantly change the world around us by being an example to those people that touch our lives. Our world will evolve when people change their ideas, thoughts, and actions. There are already millions of others who believe as we do. Quantum leaps will also occur in our evolutionary journey. Our rapidly expanding universe is the result of our creative thoughts and dominant beliefs. The rapid evolutionary development of the human brain's capacity for creative potential allows for expanded learning and knowledge and a greater awareness. However, we must first recognize the difference between the rational, analytical ego and the potential of our evolved response to creativity, intuition, and synchronicity. As we grow in knowledgeable awareness, we become multisensory in our perceptions.

There is a magical moment when we suddenly realize our true, loving identity as consciousness and our roles and purpose in life. Self-realization reflects our humility in accepting the beckoning call of the creative universe to experience love, beauty, peace, and joy. For many years, this transformation has been called *the sweet surrender*. Many will say it is the surrender to the will of the Creator, God, Tao, or Allah, with abandonment of the ego. For others, the change is simply learning to live in the flow of the creative universe. In either case, we do not have to be of any particular religious persuasion to experience the surrender. The sweet surrender will forever change our beliefs and perceptions and will therefore change our lives and our destinies. We can love all of creation unconditionally.

Just think of the infinite possibilities in our world of energies and choices. The truth is that peace and joy follow quite naturally after we realize that love and beauty are the essence of our being. It is the human ego that stands in the way of a profound realization. The ego assumes the role of gatekeeper in deciding what matters are not threatening. The ego causes doubt and reservation, and the very idea of any surrender may bring thoughts and fears of vulnerability.

Giving up so much of the self can create in us a feeling of risk—the risk of being hurt—or the fear of losing our identity. The human ego is rooted in fear and competition, and denies love. Actually, the sweet surrender to love will not cause us to lose anything but will allow us to discover something far greater.

We have discovered that we live in an electrified energy universe and that we can use our minds, our thoughts and awareness, and our consciousness to change those very small particles of energy called our body's cells. We can also use our minds to change our biology, beliefs, and intentions, to transform our lives. The next step is to discover our true inner being—which is consciousness or the soul. Body, mind, and spirit—a complete personal transformation!

There is a growing human awareness and worldview of an impending evolutionary transformation with a collective consciousness. Many of us are witnessing an increasing multisensory perception with societal awareness and behavioral changes. Many believe that the transformation of our civilization has been prompted by the rapid increase in technology, advances in quantum sciences, and the expansion of the Internet. The Internet serves as a method of social networking and distribution of information—the knowledge required to prompt our evolution. There are websites that prompt us to join the millions of other people in contributing our concentrated thought energies, our emotions, and our beliefs to a collective, convergent, and creative mass. Eventually, the growing number of people will reach a critical mass, or tipping point, and will begin a rapid worldwide transformation. Also, because they are not mutually exclusive, we will likely see a convergence of science and religion. More and more, the science of theoretical physics and quantum mechanics is clarifying and documenting the phenomenon of consciousness historically known to many religions.

Imagine what will happen when we realize and apply the implications of the energetic universe in areas of health, education, economics, and agronomics. Very likely, we could find an egalitarian life with a balance of the materialistic and the spiritual aspects. In this manner, we can also develop a maximum personal expression while also providing maximum benefits.

> *Touching hands – the silent commune of our souls.*
> *Measuring time only by the moments we share.*
> *Touch not only with your hands, but also with your heart.*
>
> —UNKNOWN

Epilogue

You are the most important person that you could ever get to know. Know who you are, know your beliefs, and know what it is that you wish to do. You are the creator of your quantum reality—the transformational experience of love and self-discovery.

In 1603, William Shakespeare wrote this in Hamlet's soliloquy: "To be or not to be, that is the question." I now ask, "Who do you choose to be?" The universe is awaiting your answer.

Thanks for being part of my reality. Have the best life ever on your journey through consciousness.

Ed Scott

About the Author

Ed Scott was raised in Minneapolis, Minnesota. He enlisted in the U.S. military after high school and traveled to Newfoundland, Portugal, Morocco, Spain, France, Germany, and England. Extensive travel with the U.S. Navy and the U.S. Army gave him the opportunity to observe many cultures and interact with people of differing religions and beliefs.

Upon returning to civilian life, Ed became a licensed police officer with the Minneapolis Police Department, where he served for thirty-six years until retirement in 1998. During those years, he attended several different churches seeking answers for personal and spiritual growth. Ed is no longer affiliated with any particular faith or worship service.

He has attended several colleges and universities across the country. For more than forty years, Ed has studied comparative religions, metaphysics, philosophy, and spirituality as they relate to human consciousness and beliefs. This search led him to become involved with the Institute for the Study of Human Awareness, where he served as president of the board for fifteen years until the year 2000. Ed has continued to be affiliated with the Institute for the Study of Human Awareness. He has also been a professional photographer, draftsman, and a licensed aircraft pilot. Ed now lives retired in northern Wisconsin.

Ed Scott has published several books through CreateSpace, an Amazon Group and Kindle Direct.

Happiness is measured not by what we have, but by what we hold dear in our heart.

—U<small>NKNOWN</small>

Made in the USA
Charleston, SC
07 November 2016